SO-AUG-246

Early Childhood Education

Problems and Methods

Early Childhood Education

Problems and Methods

Marjorie L. Hipple

University of Florida
Gainesville, Florida

GOODYEAR PUBLISHING COMPANY, INC.
Pacific Palisades, California

© Copyright 1975 by
Goodyear Publishing Company
Pacific Palisades, California 90272

All rights reserved. No part of this book may be
reproduced in any form or by any means without
permission in writing from the publisher.

Library of Congress Catalog Card Number:
75-99956

ISBN: 0-87620-230-X

Y-230X-0

Current printing (last number):
10 9 8 7 6 5 4 3 2 1

Printed in the United States of America

This book is dedicated to my husband, Ted,

and

to our children, Kathy, Bruce, and Betsy

GOODYEAR EDUCATION SERIES

Theodore W. Hipple, Editor
University of Florida

GOODYEAR EDUCATION SERIES
Theodore W. Hipple, Editor

CHANGE FOR CHILDREN
Sandra Nina Kaplan, Jo Ann Butom Kaplan, Sheila Kunishima Madsen, Bette K. Taylor

CRUCIAL ISSUES IN CONTEMPORARY EDUCATION
Theodore W. Hipple

ELEMENTARY SCHOOL TEACHING: PROBLEMS AND METHODS
Margaret Kelly Giblin

FACILITATIVE TEACHING: THEORY AND PRACTICE
Robert Myrick and Joe Wittmer

THE FOUR FACES OF TEACHING
Dorothy I. Seaberg

THE FUTURE OF EDUCATION
Theodore W. Hipple

MASTERING CLASSROOM COMMUNICATION
Dorothy Grant Hennings

THE OTHER SIDE OF THE REPORT CARD
Larry Chase

POPULAR MEDIA AND THE TEACHING OF ENGLISH
Thomas R. Giblin

RACE AND POLITICS IN SCHOOL COMMUNITY ORGANIZATIONS
Allan C. Ornstein

PERFORMING METROPOLITAN SCHOOLS
Allan Ornstein, Daniel Levine, Doxey Wilkerson

SCHOOL COUNSELING: PROBLEMS AND METHODS
Robert Hyrick and Joe Wittmer

SECONDARY SCHOOL TEACHING: PROBLEMS AND METHODS
Theodore W. Hipple

SOLVING TEACHING PROBLEMS
Mildred Bluming and Myron Dembo

TEACHING, LOVING, AND SELF-DIRECTED LEARNING
David Thatcher

VALUE CLARIFICATION IN THE CLASSROOM: A PRIMER
Doyle Casteel and Robert Stahl

WILL THE R EAL TEACHER PLEASE ST AND UP?
Mary Greer and Bonnie Rubinstein

SOCIAL STUDIES AS CONTROVERSY
R. Jerrald Shive

A YOUNG CHILD EXPERIENCES
Sandra Nina Kaplan, Jo Ann Butom Kaplan, Sheila Kunishima Madsen, Bette K. Taylor

Contents

Preface

If you are an early childhood educator or plan to become one, you are fortunate to have the opportunity to play a significant role in helping young children grow and develop. There is little doubt that early childhood experiences are of crucial importance in achieving one's potential as an adult. As a teacher of young children, you will be directly responsible for providing enriching experiences for preschoolers. This book is intended to help you develop and apply skills, knowledge, and attitudes that will produce constructive early childhood experiences and that will help you facilitate these positive learnings in young children.

This book is based on two assumptions. The first is that teaching is largely a problem-solving activity. Each day teachers make decisions about matters ranging from such simple problems as when to show a particular movie to more complex questions such as how to deal with interpersonal conflicts in the classroom. The author believes that problem-solving behaviors improve with analysis and practice. A major objective in writing this book is to help you learn to make informed decisions about problems you may face in your teaching by analyzing your responses to the sample cases presented in each chapter.

The second assumption is that most of the problems you are likely to have will not stem from a lack of knowledge about subject matter but are more likely to be questions regarding how to interact effectively with young children, how to develop early childhood programs, how to obtain and utilize educational resources, and how to work with adults—parents, staff members, and volunteers—in carrying out the program. The topics included in the five chapters of this book deal with such concerns. Although the cases do not by any means cover the universe of teaching problems, they do represent the more frustrating and pressing problems faced by early childhood educators.

The format and content of this book are designed to teach you to solve real problems in early childhood education. More than thirty cases have been selected from actual teaching experiences with preschool children to provoke your responses. Each case is part of a four-page unit. The problem is presented on the first page. On a blank page opposite the problem, you are asked to participate by writing your proposed solutions to the problem. The third page, also blank, calls for your reactions to the alternate solutions offered on the fourth page. The alternate solutions are not presented as being either correct or incorrect, nor are they arranged in an order suggesting a hierarchy of importance or value.

At the end of each chapter is a short overview of the topic. The discussion is not intended to be a comprehensive statement but rather to suggest guidelines, to offer advice, and to stimulate your thinking about yourself and your teaching. In addition, a short bibliography is included for those interested in further information on the topic.

The problems and the discussion and insights brought about by them are the basis for this book. Ideally, each case should provoke you to respond to the problems and then to analyze these responses: Why would you do thus and so? What are the potential outcomes of your actions?

The completion of a manuscript brings with it a sigh of relief that one's labors are at last at an end. The labors in this case would never have borne fruit were it not for the encouragement of my professional colleagues and college students, who helped me to solve problems and were generous about sharing their own with me. Nor would this book have gotten beyond the "thinking about" stage were it not for the love and patience of my family while it was being written. To my children, Kathy, Bruce, and Betsy, I owe my thanks for their understanding and help when Mom was "busy on the thing." But most especially, I thank my husband, Ted. He encouraged me to start the book, acted as a professional sounding board, provided unlimited assistance as my editor, and—most important—continued to live with me throughout the venture.

MARJORIE L. HIPPLE
Gainesville, Florida

one

Working with Young Children

THE STRANGE DISAPPEARANCE
OF TOMMY'S TURTLE

The day is coming to a close; boots are on, snowsuits buttoned and zipped, and you are busily gathering notes to send home with the children in your nursery school class. All at once you hear whimpers behind you. Looking back, you see four-year-old Tommy choking forth wrenching sobs. You ask him what the trouble is, but you understand little of his jerking reply until a compassionate onlooker provides the answer: "Tommy's turtle is gone!" And then you realize that the beloved turtle Tommy brought to share with the class is nowhere to be found.

Tommy had come to school this morning carrying a small aquarium filled with plants, rocks, water, and of course, Bert, the tiny green turtle. "My Uncle George gave Bert to me last Easter," Tommy proudly announced. During the day, he told the class all of his turtle's virtues, adventures, and characteristics. This turtle was clearly like no other to Tommy. As you watched the children eagerly crowd around the aquarium during the morning, you knew they, too, were thoroughly entranced by it.

And now the turtle has disappeared. You grasp at all possibilities: The toilet? The sink? The floor? You engage the children in a thorough search but turn up nothing—all against the background of Tommy's sobs, which are rapidly increasing in size and pitch.

Then you remember that Phillip, especially, spent much time admiring the turtle, and you wonder: Could Phillip have taken it? He is poor, and you doubt that he has ever owned a pet or anything of material worth. You recall the wonder in his eyes as he sat, transfixed, by the aquarium most of the day. Was he tempted, you wonder, simply to take the animal for his own?

Time is racing by. Tommy is getting hysterical. Amid the din of your thoughts and his cries, you decide you must act. What is your move?

YOUR SOLUTION

YOUR REACTIONS TO THE ALTERNATE SOLUTIONS

ALTERNATE SOLUTIONS

1. Call Phillip up to you and ask if he has taken Tommy's turtle. Demand that he return it, and, if he doesn't, search him and lecture him about stealing.

2. Do nothing. You have no proof. You can't search under all those snowsuits anyway. Tommy will survive and soon forget the incident. *C'est la vie.*

3. Tell Tommy that you will continue the search after school is out and have his turtle for him in the morning. After he leaves, run—don't walk—to the nearest pet store and purchase a turtle to impersonate the wayward one.

4. Engage the group in a discussion about the incident. Explain that Tommy will be unhappy if he must go home without his turtle. Suggest that, although everyone likes the turtle and might like to borrow it, it is time to return it to Tommy so that he can take it back to its own home. You might add that, after all, the turtle would get lonely for Tommy and its home tonight. If someone fishes out the turtle, thank him and forget the incident.

5. Ask the children if anyone has Tommy's turtle. If no one admits it, have everyone strip down. Open mouths, hands, and pockets for an on-the-spot search. If the turtle is found, talk to the children about the virtues of truthfulness and respect for the property of others. Send a note home to the parents of the guilty child, requesting a conference.

A PIDDLING PROBLEM

Danny has been in your class of four-year-olds for five months now. Until recently, you've had no cause for concern about him. He is a shy but cheerful child, who willingly participates in most of the preschool activities. He seems to be well liked by his peers, who return Danny's warmth and generosity by seeking out his company during the day. You know Danny's family and it appears to be a stable and happy one. Danny is the middle child of three. His mother and father seem to be concerned and loving parents to all of their children. In short, Danny's life at school and at home has been exceedingly normal.

About two weeks ago, Danny began to exhibit behavior that has you worried. Although he has been toilet trained for a year, he is regressing—wetting himself about every other day, it seems. You've tried to determine whether there's a pattern to the accidents or a reason for them, but none seems to exist. The accidents occur at any time of the day, without warning. Danny's temperament may be a bit more moody than it usually is, but otherwise, he seems unchanged.

You've hesitated to act, thinking that the regression was only a momentary one. You know that many times, children simply get so wrapped up in their play that they forget or wait too long to heed their natural warning signals. Further, using the toilet is not nearly so crucial to children during certain periods of their development as the more exciting activities they perform. Surely, Danny does not seem to be overly concerned about the problem. He agrees amicably about the need for a trip to the bathroom and a change of clothing each time he has an accident, announcing matter-of-factly that it's "Time for new pants!" He seems not at all disconcerted or upset about the problem. But his behavior is not improving. In fact, it's getting worse. Today, after *two* accidents, you decide that something must be done. The question, however, is what to do?

YOUR REACTIONS TO THE ALTERNATE SOLUTIONS

ALTERNATE SOLUTIONS

1. Danny's regression is probably an attention-getting device. If it continues, tell his parents that he should be withdrawn from school until he matures.

2. A kidney infection or other physical problem may be the cause of Danny's incontinence. Confer with his parents about the problem and suggest that they seek medical attention for it.

3. Ignore the relapse. It may be a brief regression that will right itself in time. You may worsen the problem by drawing attention to it.

4. An emotional problem could be causing the regression. Confer with Danny's parents about his behavior and attempt to determine whether any new factors at home could be causing him emotional distress or insecurity. Suggest that Danny's parents seek further professional help if the behavior continues.

5. Danny should know better. Explain to him that "Big boys do not wet themselves." Tell him that you expect a change in his behavior and that you will withdraw privileges, such as outdoor play, if he continues to wet himself.

6. Danny may simply get too engrossed in what he's doing to heed his physical warning system. Remind him and accompany him to the bathroom periodically. Praise him when his bathroom ventures succeed.

SUPER BRIGHT OR SUPER BRAT?

"Some men are born great; some achieve greatness; some have greatness thrust upon them." Or so goes the old saying. Gerald is one of the first variety; he was born great. Now five years old, he is without question the most precocious youngster you have ever seen.

Gerald (never "Jerry"—just ask his mother, who very pointedly corrected you when you used the nickname) has been tutored almost since birth. Though not wealthy, his bright and intellectually motivated parents have spent hour upon hour with him—reading to him, discussing sophisticated ideas with him, helping him learn to write. Quite unabashedly, they want to produce an intellectual prodigy, a genius under six.

And, from what you can gather, they have succeeded. Gerald already reads as well as most fourth graders. He talks to you like an adult. He is very inquisitive and quick to grasp even sophisticated concepts.

What bothers you about Gerald is not his intellectual development, though he does demand more than his fair share of your time. It's his social development, especially in relation to your other, mostly average children. "You're dumb!" is his favorite expression, which he uses several times a day with other children who are less quick at learning than he. Whenever you try to teach concepts inductively—relative sizes, for example, or numbers—Gerald always leaps in with the generalization before the other children even know what the problem is. Then, while you try to teach the other children, Gerald becomes bored and disruptive.

And the situation is worsening. Yesterday, Susan cried when Gerald called her "a big dumb bunny." Today he blurted out the ending of a story you were reading to your students, right after you had anticipated that someone might know the ending and requested that anyone knowing it, keep it a "secret." Tomorrow, he'll do something else. So, you think, must you.

YOUR REACTIONS TO THE ALTERNATE SOLUTIONS

ALTERNATE SOLUTIONS

1. Suggest that Gerald be withdrawn from the kindergarten and placed in a program for gifted children, which could truly challenge him.

2. Suggest that Gerald skip kindergarten and move right into first-grade work.

3. Call for a psychiatric consultation about Gerald. He is an obnoxious child. Even geniuses have to live peaceably with others. It is possible that Gerald needs psychological help.

4. Confer with Gerald's parents and suggest that they start treating him less like a prodigy and more like a child.

5. You have no problems. You ought to be delighted at the good fortune of having a Gerald come into your life. Individualize your program and use your creative talents to challenge his unusual mind.

A TALE OF ANARCHY AND HOW IT SPREAD

Robert has been having difficulty adjusting to school since the year began. He constantly interferes with the activities of other children in your kindergarten class, refuses to follow any of the classroom routines, and challenges your patience and authority constantly. Robert is bright enough; on his good days, he amazes you with his maturity. Far more often, he is so disruptive and uncooperative that he prevents the class from getting much accomplished.

At nap time, everyone rests except Robert. "Don't wanna rest," he argues. What he apparently wants to do is climb on tables and overturn chairs, or create other havoc. During free-play periods, while his peers pursue their favorite activities, Robert runs excitedly from one end of the room to the other, seldom concentrating on anything for more than a few seconds. While his classmates listen closely to a favorite selection at story time, Robert hums, nudges his neighbors, and otherwise disturbs them and you.

It is not surprising that Robert has problems in school. His family is unsupportive, poor, and transient. Robert is one of six children. The father is an unstable influence, deserting the family whenever the going gets especially rough. The mother is a sweet but ineffectual person, who is clearly overwhelmed by her problems. You have met with the mother a few times, and you know that a social worker is working with the family. Still, Robert's behavior has not changed.

You have tried several approaches in handling Robert, but nothing seems to work. Ignoring him fails. Isolating him makes him more difficult. Rewarding him for good behavior is only minimally successful. Meanwhile, the otherwise cooperative children in the class have noticed the attention Robert's antics receive, and they are beginning to imitate his behavior. Even your best students are starting to behave like anarchists. Other children, less bold, are becoming upset by your harried efforts to deal with Robert.

By January, the situation has steadily deteriorated. You realize that unless you do something quickly, your classroom will be a raving madhouse by June. But what can you do?

YOUR REACTIONS TO THE ALTERNATE SOLUTIONS

ALTERNATE SOLUTIONS

1. Remove Robert from the class. You cannot work with him at this point. Transfer him to a social adjustment class, if one exists, or suspend him and recommend that he enter kindergarten again the following year. You cannot control his home situation or other external factors that may be influencing his behavior, but you can improve the climate for the other children in your class by removing him from the group.

2. Keep trying. Don't expect miracles. Robert needs to keep interacting with you and his peers if he is to learn suitable behaviors.

3. Stop operating in a vacuum. You need help to get at the causes and reach solutions to Robert's disruptive behavior. He may have serious developmental problems. Confer with his parents and appropriate professional staff members to share insights and agree on decisions about Robert.

4. Use the situation as an opportunity to learn about democratic living. Encourage Robert and the rest of your class to discuss why such positive behavior as cooperation is necessary and desirable. Strive to develop the peer pressure and support Robert needs to improve his behavior.

DID I HEAR A MURDER PLOT
OR A FANTASIZING TOT?

You passed the housekeeping corner today and overheard the following: "I hate you, you brat. I'm going to kill you. I'll slice you up in little pieces and boil you in a pot. You're bad and ugly. I hate you, I hate you, I hate you!" As this soliloquy proceeds, you note that the child, four-year-old Jane, is actively beating a baby doll.

The gory monologue in itself does not disturb you. You know that such behavior is not terribly uncommon among preschoolers: Children often act out melodramas, tragedies, and other fantasies in their play. But Jane's behavior momentarily halts you in your tracks. She usually takes on the loving role of mother or, at worst, a mildly reproving one. In other ways, Jane has been a model of decorum all year—soft spoken, even tempered, and seldom ruffled by anything. Thus, you are somewhat shaken by the hostility in her speech.

The knowledge that Jane has recently been joined by a new baby brother does little to relieve your piece of mind. After all, until two months ago, Jane had been an only child. You shudder as you consider the literal interpretation of Jane's behavior: Is she actually rehearsing for some awful act? You worry at the symbolic interpretation that her behavior suggests: Does she feel abandoned by her parents because of the new baby's arrival? Does she hate him for taking her place? You try to shrug off your fears. "After all," you sigh, "she's probably lost in some imaginary play she's created. There's probably no cause for concern."

Still, you wonder if you should act, considering all you know, and if so, what should you do?

YOUR SOLUTION

YOUR REACTIONS TO THE ALTERNATE SOLUTIONS

ALTERNATE SOLUTIONS

1. Intervene immediately. Jane must know that aggression is not acceptable behavior in school. Tell her that nice girls do not beat baby dolls. Then show her how to care for and love the doll.

2. Ignore the incident. Play is an opportunity for children to act out their frustrations and desires. The experience may relieve any tensions Jane may have. Finally, Jane's behavior may simply be fantasizing through play rather than revealing actual feelings or events.

3. Call Jane's parents immediately. Cite Jane's behavior and tell them you are concerned about it. Let them deal with the problem if they want to.

4. Do not intervene at this time. Instead, observe Jane closely to note whether her other behavior in school is different from what is normal for her. If her other behavior has changed, confer with staff psychologists, social workers, or other appropriate personnel to determine the best course of action.

THUS SPAKE STEVEN

"Dadadaboydaboydaboy . . ." Steven is conveying an anguished message to you and waiting for your reply. From the pitch and intensity of his voice, you know that he is obviously bothered about something, yet you have no idea what that something is because you simply cannot understand a word of Steven's speech. Steven stutters, especially when he is excited. And, since he is a bright and enthusiastic four-year-old, he is excited much of the time. His questions and comments about the world are endless, even if they are not always intelligible. Steven appears to be unaware, or at least unashamed, of his communication problem. Happily, his peers have not made fun of his stuttering and, indeed, they seem better able to understand him than you do. Your aide and other adults who are occasionally in your room seldom have the remotest idea of what he is saying.

When Steven runs to you, eager to communicate, you lean close, hoping to understand whatever he is trying to say. Still, you have difficulty and often fail to know for sure what he needs or wants. You have noticed this problem for the three months Steven has attended nursery school, and you are becoming increasingly concerned about it. If it is a passing problem, you wonder whether it is wise to draw Steven's attention to it. After all, you'd rather have a stuttering communication than none at all. At the same time, you worry that you may be making it too easy for him to get what he wants without motivating him to clarify his speech.

Steven's parents seem unconcerned about his difficulty. "Stevie always makes himself understood. He points or takes me to whatever he needs if I don't understand him immediately. Don't worry, he'll grow out of it," commented his mother at your last conference. But you are not so sure. Anyway, you think it is time to stop worrying and start acting.

YOUR REACTIONS TO THE ALTERNATE SOLUTIONS

ALTERNATE SOLUTIONS

1. Ask Steven to repeat his messages until you understand them.

2. Tell Steven to stop stuttering and to speak up so that he can be understood. Do not comply with his requests until he has made them clear.

3. Refer Steven to a speech therapist for diagnosis and therapy, if therapy is indicated. If a school speech therapist is not available, suggest to Steven's parents that they seek professional help from an appropriate source in the community.

4. Draw no attention to Steven's speech. Try in whatever way possible to understand and respond to Steven's speech.

NO GIRLS (OR BOYS) ALLOWED

"Get away from here, Mary Ann. You can't play with us. We're playing trucks. Girls can't drive trucks. Go away." You are not surprised by
the diatribe Richard delivers. He and three other boys are busily maneu-
vering trucks in the sandy play-area, pretending any number of grand
schemes. And a girl just isn't about to invade their turf—not safely,
anyway.

Boys have dominated truck play in your kindergarten class, just as they
have jealously appropriated the blocks as theirs and theirs alone. You had
never thought too much about their behavior until Mary Ann tearfully ap-
proached you about the situation. "I like to play with trucks, too," she
cried. "Why can't girls play with the trucks?"

You listen to Mary Ann and examine your own values. "Why," you
ponder, "can't they?" Then you realize that not only are girls excluded
consciously or unconsciously from many tradionally "masculine" activities—playing trucks, cowboys, and so on—but boys are seldom welcomed
into such traditionally "feminine" activities as doll play and housekeeping,
which are dominated by the girls in your class. Mary Ann and a couple of
her female cohorts rule the roost in the housekeeping corner every bit as
zealously as the boys covet their trucks and blocks. It's as though certain
members of each sex had established their own unbreachable territorial
imperatives. Given the way society has liberalized traditional sex roles,
you wonder how you should handle sexist behaviors.

Meanwhile, Mary Ann still wants to play with the trucks and is impa-
tiently awaiting your response.

YOUR REACTIONS TO THE ALTERNATE SOLUTIONS

ALTERNATE SOLUTIONS

1. Redirect Mary Ann to another activity. After all, boys have their rights, too. They enjoy the male companionship associated with exclusive activities, and they need that companionship if they are to develop sex-role identification. Suggest that Mary Ann play with more congenial friends and at more ladylike activities.

2. Intervene immediately. Suggest to the boys that women do indeed drive trucks, work on road crews, and so on. Insist that Mary Ann be allowed to play with the trucks if she desires to. But be sure you intervene also when boys are excluded from activities by their female peers.

3. Let Mary Ann work out her own problems. You cannot force children to be tolerant. The boys will let her join them when they feel she adds to their group. She will only be rejected if you force her into the group.

4. Educate your class about sexism. Teach your students about the concept of role stereotypes, and in other ways develop their appreciation for sexual equality as well as sexual differences.

5. Tell Mary Ann you'll let her play with trucks with the boys if she will let Richard and the other boys play with the dolls and other toys in the housekeeping corner.

Billy finally drew blood! Considering his history you are not surprised, for this is not the first time he has had conflicts with other four-year-olds in the class. Billy wants what he wants, when he wants it. And woe to the child who stands in his way. The other day, for example, Billy tried to talk Greg out of a truck, coaxing, "Come on, Greg. You can have the blue truck over there." "No," from Greg. Then, making one more verbal attempt, Billy promised, "I'll give it back in a minute. Let me have it." Probably knowing how undependable were Billy's promises, Greg clutched the popular truck to his chest and again said, "No!" A hand shot out like an anteater's tongue, grabbed the truck, and Billy walked off with the prize. Observing all this, you had him return the truck to tearful Greg. Not all of Billy's desires are so readily won. Last week, he grabbed a jump rope Debby was using with some friends. No pushover, Debby held her ground and a tug-of-war ensued. Brawnier and more determined, Debby kept the rope.

You've worked with Billy throughout the year, trying to curb his aggression and teach him the necessity to respect the rights and desires of others. Much of the time, Billy is cooperative, but his impulsive behavior erupts again and again with a Machiavellian flair. You have known him to take three turns to each one taken by others waiting in line for an activity, since he apparently sees no purpose to the "end-of-the-line" policy when he is concerned. You've also heard complaints about his "pigging" cookies on the sly during snack time, but you have yet to catch him in the act. In short, Billy is not only a bully but a con artist as well.

Today an incident occurred that disturbed your patient resolve. Billy pushed a child who refused to share a toy with him. The toy bumped the victim sharply during the scuffle, causing a cut on the lip. Blood and tears flowed rapidly from the victim's face, while Billy stood entranced by his damage.

Although the cut is a minor one, the sight of blood is enough to make you realize that something needs to be done about Billy's behavior. You cannot permit him to bully and bruise other children, so you intervene immediately. What do you do?

YOUR SOLUTION

YOUR REACTIONS TO THE ALTERNATE SOLUTIONS

ALTERNATE SOLUTIONS

1. Confront Billy with the consequences of his behavior. As the victim sobs, scold Billy for causing the accident. Insist that he apologize; then isolate him from the group for a while.

2. Confront Billy with the consequences of his behavior. Tell him that, although you doubt that he intended physical harm, pushing and grabbing sometimes cause such harm. Ask him if he can think of any other ways to get what he wants. Suggest alternate behaviors if he cannot. Have him try alternatives with your guidance.

3. Calmly take the victim aside and administer first aid. Tell the child, in Billy's presence, that Billy did not intend to hurt him. Suggest that Billy obtain another toy or wait his turn for the toy in question.

4. Send a note home requesting a conference with Billy's parents. They need to work with him. He is in need of parental and, possibly, professional help.

5. Take the problem to your principal or other appropriate staff members.

6. Forget about it. These things happen in school. No doubt Billy is just going through a phase.

SPANK, SHAKE, SHAME . . . OR SCRAM

After school today, you sat in agony while your principal went over his evaluation of your teaching. He has visited your classroom *six* times in the last four months. As the conference proceeds, you realize why.

He began the session with the usual positive remarks: "Well, you really have a lot of enthusiasm for teaching . . . and I think you have the potential to be an outstanding teacher. But. . . ." And then he delivered a devastating evaluation of your performance. "But you can be loving, and dedicated, and conscientious, yet, unless you can get the children to behave, to follow directions, and to do what is expected of them, you cannot be an effective teacher. You have rotten classroom discipline! You know, talking and reasoning don't work with all children. Some of them—especially if they are disadvantaged as are our students—respond better to more *concrete* methods of discipline. I know you dislike using physical punishment, but some children expect it when they get out of line. Why don't you talk with your colleagues, Mrs. Jones and Mrs. Brown? They could probably give you some good tips on classroom discipline."

The punch line that culminated the evaluation still rings in your ears: "I'll be here to help you in any way I can, but you must know that, unless your classroom discipline improves, we will be unable to rehire you."

You would like to be angry at your principal, but you can't be. You *have* had problems with classroom control. It is January and you are still trying to establish some modicum of classroom order when, in the classrooms on either side of yours, peace seems to reign. Why? Because Mrs. Jones and Mrs. Brown don't fool around. When one of their students steps out of line, he or she is swiftly dealt with, either by a spanking, a shaking, or a strong verbal reprimand. Yet their students do not appear unhappy or abused.

Your approach to discipline has been to praise good behavior and to ignore or redirect inappropriate behavior. You have never used physical punishment, hoping instead that positive guidance will encourage the students to develop self-discipline. And your classroom discipline has improved. The children are beginning to exhibit some self-control and responsibility. But you still have a long way to go.

Now you have been told to shape up—or else! The thought of imitating your colleagues goes against all you have been taught and believe. Yet you are beginning to wonder whether a loving spanking may not be better than mere words with some children. Of one thing you are sure: You do not want to lose your job. But how can you save it while retaining your own integrity?

YOUR REACTIONS TO THE ALTERNATE SOLUTIONS

ALTERNATE SOLUTIONS

1. It's about time you shaped up. It sounds as if not only the children need some loving spankings, but perhaps their teacher could use one or two herself. By all means, do whatever is necessary to maintain control. After all, you are in charge.

2. Ignore your principal and continue your positive methods of guiding behavior. They may be less dramatic now but are more effective over the long haul.

3. Have you thought about a compromise? Use whatever physical punishment is necessary initially to gain the attention and respect of the children. Then, when you have the situation under control, begin to replace the physical punishment with reason and other more positive approaches.

4. Resign. If you continue to work in this school, you will either have to change your value system or be fired.

WORKING WITH YOUNG CHILDREN

A child's preschool education is important. It is important for its here-and-now aspect and what is or is not accomplished here and now. Each year of a child's life has a special value, and preschools must first of all fill each of these years with bountiful worthwhile experiences for every child. Preschool education is important also because it is *pre*school, that is, an initial experience in group living for the child, and one that may establish patterns and attitudes that persist throughout his education. As the child's teacher in his preschool experience, you have therefore the dual tasks of assuring that the here-and-now aspect promotes optimum benefits for the child and that the patterns and attitudes established are good ones.

It is difficult work, this business of being a preschool teacher. Its demands are many: patience, wisdom, warmth, compassion, humor, maturity, physical and emotional energy, to name a few. Its rewards, unfortunately, are seldom as financially attractive as those of other professions, but among the rewards must be counted heavily the enormous potential for personal satisfaction to be derived from the work you do—the sense that you have helped a child get a good start in life.

This whole book centers on how you can make the here-and-now worthwhile. (Indeed, if the present is handled well, the future will take care of itself.) Its focus is on some of the many aspects of the preschool teacher's work. It is fitting that this opening chapter deals with what may very well be the most important of these aspects—the interactions between you and the children you teach. Such interactions are at the core of preschool education. Their quality may enrich or discourage the social, emotional, and intellectual growth of your students. Because it is to your students that you owe both your first allegiance and your best efforts, it becomes crucial that you explore the ways to effect sound interactions. This chapter discusses some of these ways.

Interactions, by definition, involve more than one person. As the term is used here, interactions involve you and one or more of your students.

As the author of this book, I have neither control over nor any means of influencing the students with whom you will interact. I do hope, however, that my words will help inform your judgments about your part in the process of interaction.

The interactions between you and your students will take a variety of forms. Sometimes you may lead your entire class in learning a song. Sometimes you may work with one or two students as they struggle to rebuild a collapsed block construction. Sometimes you may stimulate a single child to discover a new concept, to savor a new taste, to feel a new sensation, or even to make a new friend. Often, too, you will interact in affective ways, as when you help students solve social problems they have with each other. And sometimes your interactions will be silent, those of the interested onlooker, the person whose involvement is not with, but near, the children as they go about their tasks.

From your point of view, sound interactions depend basically on (1) your knowing about children in general and, what is more important, about the children you teach in particular, and (2) your knowing about yourself, especially the "self" that is a preschool teacher.

What should you know about young children? This question permits, even demands, an oversimplified answer: everything you possibly can know, and then some. Taken as a group, children of a given age have various characteristics in common, giving rise to descriptions that are familiar to most of us: "terrible twos," "trusting threes," "frustrating fours," and so forth. A general understanding of child development is vital. Lacking this knowledge, you may unwittingly fail to challenge some children or you may push others beyond their developmental limits. Worse, you might exacerbate a developmental problem rather than recognize it and attempt to effect its solution. If you do not already possess this broad base of information, acquire it. Please acquire it. It will prove invaluable in teaching young children. The books listed in the bibliography at the end of this chapter will provide a helpful starting point.

However, there remains a problem with studying common characteristics: Children are seldom "taken as a total group." They are unique individuals who have dissimilarities as pronounced as their similarities. Bruce, you will soon discover, will win you over with his half-shy smile, evoked from a frightening but diminishing sense of timidity. Kathy is bold, aggressive, demanding—and an absolute delight. Betsy already speaks in elaborately constructed sentences, while James is virtually monosyllabic in all of his utterances. Lynn, her eyes awash with the glitter of discovery, proudly reveals her latest drawing. Tommy—well, he's just Tommy. All of these differences may sometimes prove frustrating. Most teachers occasionally dream idly of how nice it would be were their students more alike, their classes more homogeneous. But such fantasies and the frustrations that produce them soon fade, when confronted with the joy, the challenge, and the spontaneity derived from the children who *are*. It is their differences that count and provide rewards for the caring teacher. You will discover, when you get to know your children as individuals, that even your most cautious generalizations about them are just that—generalizations—which must be accorded the proverbial grain of salt.

Many means exist for you to get to know your students. Indeed, you will find that you know them better today than you did yesterday, better this month than last. Observations, both formal and informal, help. Choose a particular child and watch him as he works alone and with others. What is he doing? How does he seem to feel about what he is doing? How is he responding to others? How are they responding to him? You can record your observations in several ways. Checklists of behaviors, for instance, are easily kept and provide an ongoing view of the child. You might also keep anecdotal records of what you observe. Although requiring greater time and effort, such records can provide information that is not readily available in other forms.

But each child is more than his classroom behavior indicates. He is a product of, and a contributor to, a home environment, which you should try to get to know. What are things like in his home? Is it a stable, warm, and supportive environment? How can his parents be encouraged to enhance their child's school experience? It is often difficult to learn with conviction anything substantial about a child's home life and, therefore, inferences must be cautiously drawn. Still, you should try to learn what you can. Meetings with the parents, in the home or the school, or, if necessary, by telephone can provide you with a start.

Similarly, some knowledge of a child's culture is essential for understanding his motivations and behavior. If you are not already a member of his culture, you should try hard to become familiar with it. You may have heard the story of the young child who was thought to be disrespectful to his teacher because he turned away from her when she spoke directly to him. Yet in his culture, turning away so that one's ear, not one's eye, pointed at the speaker was the highest form of respect. The folkways and mores of a particular culture have a profound and pervasive effect on behavior, even that of young children. Your understanding will pay dividends.

Knowing your children, then, will facilitate your producing sound interactions with them. But this is only half the knowledge you need. You must also know yourself, to know what you believe in relation to teaching young children. What are your beliefs about them and about their education? These beliefs will have an important bearing on the kinds of interactions you have with your students.

For example, there is evidence to support the contention that what you expect from children is what you get from them. "As ye sow, so shall ye reap." If you believe that your students can perform well, they are more likely to perform well than if you hold low expectations for them. The reasons for this theoretical relationship between teacher expectations and student performance are not altogether clear. Yet the theory, often referred to as a self-fulfilling prophecy or a "Pygmalion effect," is supported by research (see *Pygmalion in the Classroom*). It may be that teachers consciously or unconsciously express beliefs about the capabilities of their students as they interact with them. The children perceive these feelings and try to live up to them. It pays, then, to hold high expectations for your students.

Your beliefs about the goals of preschool education—your philosophy of education—can also influence your interactions. Long philosophical statements about the purposes of preschool education abound in books of greater length and breadth than this one is intended to have, and you should familiarize yourself with some of these. Some educational philosophies differ markedly from others. It would be presumptuous to insist that you hold to a particular set of tenets as though these had been chiseled in stone for all to follow, forever and ever, amen. What is more important is that your philosophy of education be informed and dynamic, and that it reflect the best of what is currently being thought and written.

It is imperative, however, that you clarify your own values sufficiently well to carry them through in the classroom. Your relationships with young children should be based on goals that you believe in, that you can articulate, and that you can defend. For example, as you work with young children, you might want to ask yourself questions such as these: If I believe in democratic decision making, how much do I let my students participate in decisions affecting our work together? If I value divergent thinking and creativity, what provisions do I make for unusual or unique responses? If I want to support autonomous personal behavior, how do I encourage and reward independence in my students? Although systems of philosophic beliefs cannot always be translated directly into classroom practice, belief and practice should at least not be inconsistent.

Finally, your interactions with children will be influenced by your feelings about yourself. How do you feel about yourself? If you perceive yourself as a secure, worthy, and accepted person, you will interact differently with young children than you would if you felt insecure, unworthy, and unaccepted. It is difficult to imagine a very successful teacher who has pervasive and all-consuming preoccupations with his or her own problems.

The personal attitudes you convey, the feelings about yourself that you sincerely hold and project, should be as positive as possible as often as possible. All children need and deserve the warm, confident, empathic guidance that adults, who are themselves mature in their social and emotional development, can provide. An anonymous poet put it well:

> No printed word nor spoken plea
> Can teach young minds what men should be,
> Not all the books on all the shelves
> But what the teachers are themselves.

The challenge, then, and it is a demanding one—easier to read about than to meet—is to know your children and yourself. In truth, the former is inescapable. You will learn about your children. But consciously working for this knowledge will make its acquisition more useful. The latter, learning about yourself, requires a degree of introspection not present in all people. It requires that you ask yourself who you are and why. It requires especially that you identify the "self" in you that teaches young children. Once these twin pieces of knowledge are joined, successful interactions with young children are not only possible, they are inevitable.

FOR FURTHER READING

Caldwell, Bettye M. "On Designing Supplementary Environments for Early Child Development." In *As the Twig Is Bent*, edited by Robert H. Anderson and Harold G. Shane. Boston: Houghton Mifflin, 1971.

Carswell, Evelyn M. and Roubinek, Darrell L. *Open Sesame: A Primer in Open Education*. Pacific Palisades, Calif.: Goodyear, 1974.

Combs, Arthur W., ed. *Perceiving, Behaving, Becoming*. 1962 Yearbook of the Association for Supervision and Curriculum Development. Washington, D.C.: ASCD, 1962.

Educational Policies Commission of the National Education Association and the American Association of School Administrators. "Universal Opportunities for Early Childhood Education." In *Early Childhood*

Education Rediscovered, edited by Joe L. Frost. New York: Holt, Rinehart and Winston, 1968.

Erikson, Erik. "A Healthy Personality for Every Child." In *As the Twig Is Bent*, edited by Robert H. Anderson and Harold G. Shane. Boston: Houghton Mifflin, 1971.

Grotberg, Edith, ed. *Day Care: Resources for Decisions*. Washington, D.C.: Day Care and Child Development Council of America, 1971.

Hymes, James L. *The Child under Six*. Englewood Cliffs, N.J.: Prentice-Hall, 1963.

Jersild, Arthur T. *When Teachers Face Themselves*. New York: Columbia University Press, 1968.

Leeper, Sarah Hammond; Dales, Ruth J.; Skipper, Dora Sikes; and Witherspoon, Ralph L. *Good Schools for Young Children*. Chs. 2-5. New York: Macmillan, 1974.

Maier, Henry W. *Three Theories of Child Development*. New York: Harper and Row, 1969.

Mukerji, Rose. "Roots in Early Childhood for Continuous Learning." *Young Children*, 1965, 20:343-350.

Mussen, Paul; Conger, John; and Kagan, Jerome. *Child Development and Personality*. New York: Harper and Row, 1969.

Rosenthal, Robert, and Jacobson, Lenore. *Pygmalion in the Classroom: Teacher Expectation and Pupils' Intellectual Development*. New York: Holt, Rinehart and Winston, 1968.

Silberman, Charles E. *Crisis in the Classroom*. New York: Random House, 1970.

two

Working with the Curriculum

IN THE BEGINNING WAS . . . CHAOS

Here it is! The first day of school for you and your kindergartners—and you are terrified. You've had this morning planned ever since you got this job—your first teaching position. First you would have an opening activity in which you would introduce yourself and teach a few songs and, perhaps, a nursery rhyme or two. Then you would move on to the other carefully planned activities, which you were sure the children would love.

But now, as you sense the varied emotions and observe the behaviors of the children who crowd into your room, you begin to wonder whether anything constructive will happen. One little girl is clinging to her mother's skirt, apparently frightened. Another is screaming uncontrollably as her mother turns to leave. Three boys, obviously friends, are pushing and shoving as they chase one another around the room, undaunted by their new surroundings. Defying their parents' efforts to budge them, several awestruck youngsters remain at the door.

Chaos reigns and you must somehow act calmly in the face of this un-anticipated crisis—all this in full view of several curious parents who have remained to see their youngsters off to a healthy beginning. You are as scared, embarrassed, and nonplussed as your students, but decide to try to display a calm you don't feel. You call the children to come and sit on the little rug before the piano to begin the day as planned, but nothing happens.

What now, teacher?

YOUR REACTIONS TO THE ALTERNATE SOLUTIONS

ALTERNATE SOLUTIONS

1. Forget the planned opening activity. Your students are too overstimulated and awed to appreciate it. Let them carry on. They'll eventually
calm down.

2. Have the remaining parents bring the youngsters to the rug and, if possible, sit with them until the planned activity is under way.

3. Raise your voice until it is heard. Shout if necessary to get things
under way.

4. First, approach the disrupting boys. Talk quietly with them about
how excited everyone is but stress that chasing each other in school
will hurt someone and is therefore not allowed. Suggest that later
they can go outside to run. Find an activity to occupy them and move
on to other children, welcoming them individually and involving them
in various interest centers you have set up around the room.

5. Quit your job. You are not cut out for this kind of work.

Your palms are clammy. Your heart thumps as you sit facing three awe-inspiring men. An inquisition? No, it is the interview for your first job, the one you've fervently prayed and planned for. The school has a good reputation and the salary is generous. As one of your interviewers describes the job, your excitement mounts. You know that you want it and you believe you can do it well. Your training has been good. You like children and think that you'll enjoy teaching them, and that they will enjoy and profit from your teaching. Your practice teaching was very successful, a wonderful period of challenge, excitement, and reward.

Prior to the interview, you had tried to prepare for it by posing potential questions to yourself and answering them with poise and acumen. But now, one of your interviewers—the one whose smile you suspect hides all sorts of calculated motives—asks some questions that you had never anticipated: "What, if anything, is the value of play for young children? Does play have a place in the kindergarten program and, if so, how big a place should it have?"

You are stunned. Somehow, during all of your training in early childhood education, you had always taken free play for granted. You know that ever since the time of Froebel, free play has been valued and incorporated into early childhood curricula. You have never questioned or tried to defend the value of play.

But your interviewer awaits and, so, perhaps, may your job. Mind racing, you cough, playing for time, as you gather your resources. You breathe deeply and say, . . .

YOUR SOLUTION

YOUR REACTIONS TO THE ALTERNATE SOLUTIONS

ALTERNATE SOLUTIONS

1. "Free play is not necessarily valuable for all children. It may have less value for disadvantaged children, for instance. These children may need more structured and compensatory activities than do their more advantaged peers. Even for advantaged children, free play can be overdone. The major benefits of free play can often be achieved through structured learning activities. Anyway, most children coming to school have numerous opportunities for free play at home. . . ."

2. "There is little time during a half-day program to allow for much free play. Children need the intellectual challenge that comes from more structured activities or lessons. If children get all of their work done and time allows, they should, of course, be given time to relax by pursuing play activities. . . ."

3. "Free play is valuable for *all* children and should comprise an adequate share of the school program. Through play, children can work out their intellectual, socioemotional, and physical problems at their own rate and in their own style. Free play encourages individual growth and development in ways that are not possible using direct instruction. . . ."

4. "There is little value to free play. Structured play, in which teachers direct activities to meet specific goals, is more valuable. For example, when teachers structure games to teach specific concepts, children can not only have fun but can learn at the same time. . . ."

5. "Both free play and structured activities are valuable and each has a place in the kindergarten program. Many concepts are effectively learned through intrinsic problem solving or discovery, as children work with peers, ideas, and objects during free play. On the other hand, children also learn much through external intervention or instruction from the teacher. . . ."

6. "That's a good question, one I really hadn't thought much about. How much play do you three think there ought to be in the kindergarten program?"

A TIME TO STOP, A TIME TO GO

You enjoy teaching the four-year-olds in your nursery school class. They are lively, curious, and generally fun to work with. It is not difficult to plan interesting activities for them, since they seem to enjoy themselves at almost everything they do in school. They listen raptly to stories, clamoring for more; they use creative imagination in their play; and they work exceedingly well with one another.

Your problem is not implementing stimulating activities, then, but getting the children to move from one activity to another. Transitions between activities are, in a word, *terrible.* During the transition periods, the children appear to be at their worst. Transitions seem to take forever and, inevitably, fights or accidents seem to occur. Some children object to halting projects that are half finished; others drop their work quickly without storing or cleaning up the materials they have been using.

These are the times that try not only your voice but your nerves as well, while you attempt to keep things moving. Once the children are finally settled into an activity, all goes well—until the time arrives to move on to the next. You and the children would have such beautiful times together if only something could be done about the intervals between activities. As it is, you are not satisfied with either your behavior or theirs during these frustrating periods.

You've isolated the problem. Now, how do you solve it?

YOUR REACTIONS TO THE ALTERNATE SOLUTIONS

ALTERNATE SOLUTIONS

1. Insist that the children stop whatever they are doing whenever you tell them to finish their activities. Admonish children who linger and praise those who don't.

2. Permit longer, more relaxed periods for children to conclude their activities before moving on to new ones. Warn the children to prepare to finish a few minutes before their current activity is scheduled to cease.

3. Develop and use cues to signal the transition. Play a few notes on the piano, blink the lights, or use some other consistent technique that the children can learn to recognize and heed as a cue to finish their work and prepare to move on.

4. Review your daily schedule to determine whether it permits smooth transitions. If the children are being shifted about constantly, you need to evaluate and modify your schedule.

5. Discuss with your class the need to finish activities and move on to others. Encourage an understanding of why cooperation is necessary, with the hope that ultimately, the children will exercise self-discipline in making smooth transitions between activities.

A STUDY IN BLACK AND WHITE

You are teaching an all-white kindergarten class when you receive word that a new student, a black boy, is to enroll the following week. The school in which you teach has a fairly heterogeneous mixture of socio-economic groups including children of business executives, teachers, laborers, and welfare recipients. But the community is not racially integrated nor has the school been until this year. Although to date, racial integration in the school has been slight, there is evidence of tension among the staff and students. Conversations in the teachers' lounge center on various integration problems. And you've observed on the playground and in the hallways the ostracism, name calling, and other negative behaviors noted by your colleagues who teach integrated classes in your building. On the other hand, you have also begun to notice friendships slowly emerging between white and black students.

Because you feel strongly that all humans should be welcomed and accepted in our society, you cannot tolerate discrimination of any kind. And that is why you are worried. You do not want the new student to be ill-treated in your classroom. What can you do, you wonder, to ensure that his entrance into and membership in your class will be a happy one?

YOUR REACTIONS TO THE ALTERNATE SOLUTIONS

ALTERNATE SOLUTIONS

1. Tell the class that they are to have a new classmate who is black. Carefully explain that though his color is different, he is just like them in every other way. You might discuss different hair and eye colors as examples of interesting human differences. Explain that you expect each child to be especially nice to the newcomer, just as they would be to any new student, lest he be made to feel unwelcome.

2. Send notes home to the parents of your students, explaining the situation and urging them to support the integration of the new student by counseling their children prior to his arrival.

3. Do nothing in advance of the child's arrival. Welcome him and treat him as you would any newcomer.

4. Talk with your principal to see whether the child might not be more comfortable in a classroom that already has other black students.

5. Do nothing in advance of the child's arrival. When he comes, teach concepts of equality, tolerance, and so on as part of a social studies unit, personalizing the lessons by referring to your own classroom situation.

ALL DRESSED UP WITH NO PLACE TO GO

You and your twenty-five kindergartners have made plans for a field trip to the farm. The trip is eagerly anticipated and the day for it has arrived. You expect to leave at 9 o'clock this morning. You've asked four mothers to accompany you to provide transportation and supervision for the children. This has been your normal procedure in the past and it has always worked well, the parents cooperating fully in meeting your requests. You've prided yourself on the many interesting trips your children have taken because of your careful and ambitious planning. But today your string of good fortune has been broken. At 8:15 A.M., you were informed by the school secretary that two of the mothers had called to say that they would be unable to go because of illness in their families.

Feeling angry and frustrated, you wonder why the mothers waited so long to call. Couldn't they have reached you last night, in time to line up alternate drivers? You hurriedly instruct the secretary to call other mothers to serve as replacements. At 8:45, she tells you that none of the other mothers can come today.

You look at the excited group before you; you smell the bag lunches eagerly prepared; you note the faces especially well-scrubbed for the occasion. The thought of disappointing the children fills you with despair. Then you think about how hard you worked, contacting people, setting dates, getting parental permissions, and praying for good weather. Was this all for naught? You don't even want to think about the problems you will have if you must postpone and replan the trip.

What can you do under the circumstances?

YOUR SOLUTION

YOUR REACTIONS TO THE ALTERNATE SOLUTIONS

ALTERNATE SOLUTIONS

1. Go ahead with the trip. Three adults can probably handle the situation. Although you'll no doubt be crowded in the cars, the children won't mind.

2. To venture forth with only three adults and as many cars is at best foolish and at worst irresponsible. Forget the trip. Tell the children about the change of plans and make arrangements for another day.

3. Don't give up so readily. Perhaps your secretary, your principal, or other school personnel can help out in the crisis.

4. You cannot go to the farm with inadequate transportation and supervision, but you can do something closer at hand. Take the children on a surprise field trip—a picnic to a nearby park or a visit to someone's home—for which fewer cars and supervisory adults are needed.

5. Why didn't you prepare for the problem in advance? You should have had contingency plans ready. Learn a lesson and make sure that you are fully prepared for your next trip. For the present, abandon the field trip and make the best of a bad situation.

JINGLE, JANGLE, JUNGLE

You've had a rough morning, and now, with your kindergarten students bundled up and on their way home, you have a few minutes for reflection. This is your first teaching experience and frankly, you're beginning to wonder whether you are cut out to be an early childhood teacher.

You have taught the children for three months, and somehow they have not grown the way you feel they should have. Each day they arrive filled with energy and enthusiasm, but often, before your half-day session has ended, the mood of the group has changed markedly: The children become cantankerous and moody, fight with each other, and in a few cases, throw raging temper tantrums.

Today was typical. Moods grew worse during the morning, and by the time the session ended, the children were on edge and eager to leave. And you felt guilty at being relieved to see them leave.

You look back on the morning, trying to pinpoint the trouble. At 8:30, you began an opening activity during which the children shared news, new toys, and so forth. You sang a few songs, then worked on a structured language arts activity dealing with the concepts "big" and "little." At 9 o'clock, the children worked at play activities of their own choice, which were set up about the room. At 9:30, you called the children together to work on math skills. Today they worked on identifying geometric shapes on the blackboard, following which they completed worksheets on the topic. Some children had difficulty completing the sheets. Others worked quickly and were then allowed to rest their heads on the tables until everyone was finished. At 10:15, the children cleaned up, went to the bathroom, and returned for a snack. They were rather slow, but you hurried them along to make time for the story you had planned. You noted a rash of fighting during the cleanup period and intervened to stop it.

At 10:40, you told a story that you thought the children would enjoy. Shortly after beginning the story, you realized that the group was restive. You demanded their attention, isolated children who were acting out, and continued the story until you had finished it. At 11:15, you had intended to have the children play outdoors, but you decided that the fighting would probably worsen, so you had them rest instead. During the rest period, you thought you heard some sniffles, but you couldn't locate their origin.

After resting, the children ran for their coats, tripping, shoving, and generally anxious to leave. But why? You had worked so hard to create a happy learning environment. Yet the children seem to be neither happy nor learning. What can the problem be?

YOUR SOLUTION

YOUR REACTIONS TO THE ALTERNATE SOLUTIONS

ALTERNATE SOLUTIONS

1. There are probably personality clashes among members of the group. Try to identify the children who do not get along together and intervene to establish better interpersonal relationships.

2. The children are probably reacting to the lack of structure in the curriculum. They may become overstimulated during the free-play period. Substitute a structured activity for this half-hour until you feel that the problems have subsided.

3. You may need additional help with group instruction. Ask your principal for the use of a paraprofessional to help you carry out your plans.

4. The children are probably reacting to too much structure in the curriculum. Increase the opportunities for free play and shorten or omit some of the more structured activities.

5. Your schedule is poorly arranged. Change it so that you begin the day with a story. Stories calm children down. You would then have a happier group to work with for the rest of the day.

CAN THIS PACKAGE BE RETURNED?

Your school district has invested a large sum of money in an expensive packaged curriculum in language arts. You were not yet employed as a teacher when the decision was made, but you attempt to follow the program faithfully, as you have been requested to do. Your principal is sold on the curriculum.

Midway through the year, you take stock of the situation. After evaluating the success of the curriculum in relation to student growth, you realize that it is not working. The curriculum requires heavily structured work, for which many of your children are not yet ready. Further, the goals of the curriculum are too narrow for the needs of your group. Much time is spent on eliciting from the children preestablished responses, and you believe the time could be better spent developing overall language growth, as an ongoing part of the total program. Furthermore, the children are bored by the curriculum—you note the glazed eyes and general listlessness that pervades the group during the packaged lessons.

During the last two weeks, you have been evaluating the success of the curriculum in more specific ways. You measured each student's language growth, using a checklist of specific skills that the curriculum is designed to develop. As you could have predicted from your informal observations, most of the children performed poorly. You want to change the language arts curriculum but fear that the administration will be opposed. How should you proceed?

YOUR SOLUTION

YOUR REACTIONS TO THE ALTERNATE SOLUTIONS

ALTERNATE SOLUTIONS

1. This is not a big problem. Simply drop the packaged program and do your own thing. You know best the needs of the children in your class.

2. Modify the packaged program. Use what is appropriate and adaptable to your needs. Ignore what is unsuitable for your children.

3. Take your problem to the administration. Suggest an alternate approach and defend it. If you are not supported, proceed with the packaged program, despite your qualms. The administration should know what it is doing.

4. Discuss the problem with your administration and, if possible, your colleagues. Offer to carry out an alternate curriculum on an experimental basis to determine which method encourages greater language growth.

5. The problem may not lie in the curriculum but in *your* instructional methods. Seek help from your colleagues or supervisors, if necessary, to improve your understanding of the program *and* your effectiveness in carrying it out.

ALAS, POOR HERBERT, WE KNEW HIM

Herbert was the class guinea pig. You and your four-year-olds had long since accepted Herbert as a valuable addition to the classroom. He came to school six months ago, a gift from a joyous marriage of the two guinea pigs in the first grade down the hall. From the first, he was cuddled, kissed, pulled in wagons, carried in pails, and fed all kinds of edible and sometimes dubious foods. On weekends, Herbert travelled homeward with different students in the class, who eagerly volunteered to give him weekend care. He was, in short, a beloved member of the class—almost a class mascot. It was a rare child who didn't each day show Herbert some attention—petting him, feeding him, playing with him. Even you had come to regard Herbert as a splendid little animal.

This morning as usual you looked in on Herbert. He seemed a little sluggish, his normal scurrying slowed to a languid crawl. You assumed he had had a rough night or a slight cold and thought no more about him.

A few minutes ago, a little girl came running to you, followed closely by a group of puzzled classmates. Her eyes wide, she blurted excitedly: "Something's wrong with Herbert. He won't move or play with me!" You sensed that she was about to cry and, checking again on Herbert, suddenly realized that he was neither sick nor tired. Herbert had died.

Surprisingly, the subject of death had never before come up in your classroom, and you've never thought about how you would handle it if and when it did. Yet now, as you look at Herbert's inert body and meet the questioning eyes of your students, you know you must say something. But what?

YOUR SOLUTION

YOUR REACTIONS TO THE ALTERNATE SOLUTIONS

ALTERNATE SOLUTIONS

1. Tell the children that Herbert is sleeping. Remove him surreptitiously at your earliest opportunity and replace him with a suitable double the next day.

2. Tell the children that Herbert is dead. Calm them down and cheer them up by telling them not to worry, you'll get them a new guinea pig.

3. Discuss Herbert's death with the children. Talk about the naturalness and the meaning of death. Help the children decide what to do about the guinea pig and ask whether they wish to replace it.

4. Do not discuss the matter. The children are too young to understand death. They'll only get upset and confused. Say that Herbert is sleeping. When tomorrow comes, make some excuse for his absence.

5. Tell the children that Herbert is dead. Discourage further discussion by suggesting that they talk with their parents about the matter when they get home from school.

WORKING WITH THE CURRICULUM

As a preschool teacher, you may work in a kindergarten, a nursery school, a Head Start or day-care program, or some other program in early childhood education. Whatever the school's organization, your central task will be the same: to stimulate optimal growth and development in young children. You are not simply a baby-sitter or a caretaker. Rather, you are a facilitator of learning. Indeed, you are an educator.

Again, no matter what the organization of the program in which you work, it is vital to remember that all preschools educate. Even programs that advertise themselves as offering mainly "custodial" child care do indeed educate. To deny that custodial programs educate is to ignore the fact that children always learn from their environment, regardless of its title. The question, then, is not which kinds of schools educate. They all do. The important issue is the quality of that education.

Whether that education is good or bad depends to a major degree on you. The burden, the responsibility, is yours. The purpose of this section is to offer advice that may better enable you to meet this responsibility as effectively as you can. Specifically, this section will focus on how you can develop a systematic and balanced preschool program. It will also offer some specific advice on the "special days" that add an important dimension to the preschoolers' experiences.

A GOOD PRESCHOOL PROGRAM IS SYSTEMATIC

A systematic approach to any educational program is based on a logical and dynamic interaction among the three major components of every instructional process: (1) conceptualizing objectives, (2) implementing activities to achieve these objectives, and (3) evaluating the degree to which the objectives have been achieved. The blending of these three components, their merger, systematizes an educational program. If any of the three is short-changed or ignored entirely, the whole scheme suffers.

All too often, the major focus in many preschools is on generating activities—sometimes, it seems, simply for their own sake. The purposes of the activities are either ignored or called forth after the activities have been completed. Evaluation, when it occurs, often bears little relation to the objectives or, in some cases, to the instruction. It is as though the teachers in such schools were preoccupied with simply keeping their students busy, and never mind why. These teachers are engaged in a "Now what?" kind of teaching: "Now that I've done that, what will I do next?"

Each of the components that together define the system—developing objectives, choosing activities, and evaluating—merits closer scrutiny. Because the components are so closely entwined, however, it is difficult to separate them even for purposes of discussion. But let us try, anyway.

Objectives. Objectives are of many types. Some have to do with specific and immediately observable behaviors, whereas others center on developing attitudes or habits that may or may not manifest themselves in observable behaviors for months or years to come.

It is easier to work with the former, observable, kind. For example, here are three sample objectives a preschool teacher might design. (1) The children will dress and undress themselves without excessive or unnecessary help from others. (2) The children will share classroom equipment with their peers. (3) The children will discriminate among initial consonant sounds. In each of these objectives, the children's behavior will indicate the degree to which the objective has been achieved. The word *degree*, as used here, is important. When thinking of objectives for your entire class, you must realize that not all of your children will achieve them to the same extent or in the same amount of time. Some will dress and undress themselves almost entirely without help early in the year; others will require less and less help as the year progresses; and perhaps others will still require a great deal of help at the end of the year. Further, even using objectives for individual children, the child's degree of achievement may vary from day to day. On some days, Susan willingly shares the materials in the housekeeping corner; on other days she does not. Your hope is that more of the former kinds of days will occur as the school year progresses.

Objectives having to do with attitudes, values, feelings, and the like will prove difficult to achieve, and it will be even more difficult to assess to what degree they have been achieved. For example, consider the following sample objectives. (1) The children will develop positive self-concepts. (2) The children will value schooling and learning. (3) The children will tolerate human differences. Objectives of this type seldom produce a specific, overt, observable behavior to let you know that the objective has been, or is in the process of being, achieved. Nonetheless, these are important objectives and you should try to structure activities to help reach them—even though they may defy objective and immediate measurement.

Instructional Activities. The range of activities in a typical preschool educational program could be described along a continuum—from teacher-directed or teacher-centered activities at one end, to child-directed or child-centered activities at the other. Both kinds of activities, as well as those that combine the two extremes, are very important and should be provided for in your educational program.

Child-directed activities permit children to explore their environment, to deal with concepts at their own level of development, and generally to work at their own pace. Free-play activities such as block construction provide a good example of child-directed activities. Of course, your having the blocks in your classroom indicates that you have some part in this activity, but the children are "center stage" while they work with the blocks. They select, pursue, and influence the direction that the use of the blocks takes; the blocks become their world. The choice of building a skyscraper or a low, wide building or a maze or a fort or any other imaginative construction is up to them. The activity evolves from *their* intents and imaginations.

Sometimes you will want to engage in direct instruction with one or more of your students, though seldom with either the intensity or the formality commonly found in classes of older children. At such times, you will structure activities with yourself at their center, to provide specific enrichment or remediation experiences. Many language arts activities such as story telling or finger plays are teacher directed, as is the activity of helping the children learn a new song or understand a geometric concept, such as "bigness." Not always will such activities require the attention of the entire class at the same time. You will frequently find that teacher-directed activities work most successfully with small groups of children or even with only one child.

The number and kind of different activities available for preschool classrooms virtually staggers the imagination. The following are a few examples: (1) dramatic activities in which children play at various roles, stimulated by puppets and dolls, costumes, and other equipment found throughout the room; (2) construction activities, such as block building and sand play; (3) sensorimotor manipulative activities, such as stringing beads or putting together puzzles; (4) larger motor experiences, such as climbing, running, skipping, and riding wheel toys; (5) creative art and music activities, such as painting, drawing, singing, dancing, and playing rhythm instruments; (6) experiences in science, math, or language arts, which occur in both child- and teacher-directed activities; (7) routines for developing healthy personal and social habits and attitudes, such as rest, cleanup, and snack routines, which may occur during each day.

Such a list, including lengthy explanations and/or justifications for each activity, could continue almost ad infinitum. Suffice it to say that you will not suffer from having too few activities for your students. It is important, however, that you select and arrange activities that will achieve your carefully considered objectives while also meeting your students' needs.

Evaluation. Of the three components in the instructional process, evaluation is probably the most neglected. Perhaps because preschool children appear too young to undergo the types of testing and measurement employed with older children, this is especially true in preschool education. Obviously, a four-year-old can't take a true-false test or write an essay to indicate his or her knowledge or skills. Frankly, the objectives of preschool programs are often so loosely conceptualized that they defy evaluation of any kind. Nonetheless, evaluation is as important in preschool education as at any other level of education. There is simply no excuse for not attempting to evaluate whether your objectives have been achieved. How else will you know whether your instruction has been effective?

The means you can employ in making your evaluations—that is, determining how well the activities you have designed have helped you to achieve your objectives—are many and varied. The following are only a few examples.

Performance tests can be administered successfully to preschool children. Such tests may be obtained from commercial sources and are often standardized. In most cases, however, you will want to develop your own tests to focus on your particular objectives. These may be paper-and-pencil tests, which can be administered to a group of children by a teacher or an aide. For example, the children might be asked to "Draw a circle around the picture of the biggest house" or to "Mark an X on the one dog that is different from the others." In addition, there are individual tests, which may call for simple responses from a child to indicate his knowledge or skill. The child could be required to point to the correct response, to say it, or to otherwise demonstrate it in some way requiring neither reading nor writing. Both kinds of tests can indicate how well you have achieved specific learning objectives as well as offering diagnostic information ("Johnny has trouble identifying the 'B' sound") that can help you revise objectives and formulate other instructional activities.

Checklists may also be helpful for evaluating the achievement of objectives. Like performance tests, checklists may be obtained from commercial sources or developed by you for your own purposes. Included among the items on such a list might be some of the following: "Cleans up after play," "Takes turns at group play activities," "Follows directions," "Listens attentively to stories," and so forth. Like performance tests, these checklists evaluate past learnings and diagnose future needs.

Ongoing instructional activities often have evaluation built in. When you ask Mary to give you a word beginning with the "B" sound, her response provides you with some information for evaluation and keeps the activity going. Other times, you may give specific directions that suggest evaluation. For example, when you tell children that it is time to put their materials away, their doing so or failing to do so provides you with evaluative information.

Informal observations of students are a source of information for evaluation. You will discover that you learn more about Jimmy daily—how quickly he adapts to new or different environments, how ably he learns new songs, how readily he participates. Such bits and pieces of information, acquired without any conscious intention on your part, provide an important source of data for evaluation. Sometimes you will want to plan such evaluations. Today you may try to focus on Janice: Does she seem happy? What toys does she play with during free-play time? How does she respond at story time? It is a good idea to focus your attention every so often on a particular child to discover how that child is progressing.

Finally, you should collect and analyze representative products of your students' work during the year. Does the drawing Teddy made today show any greater detail than the one he completed last month? Products such as a sandpile creation are often impermanent and, therefore, you may wish to make a record of some of them. For example, photograph the block constructions children complete or tape-record their conversations with you over the course of the year, and you will be surprised at your students' growth.

In essence, then, your approach to ensuring that your preschool program is systematic comes down to your use of objectives, instructional activities, and evaluation procedures. Ask yourself the following questions:

What objectives do I want my children to achieve? What activities, both teacher-directed and child-directed, will I provide to ensure that achievement? What means of evaluation will I employ to measure the degree of that achievement?

A GOOD PRESCHOOL PROGRAM IS BALANCED

A balanced preschool program provides activities covering many developmental areas rather than narrowly focusing on one, such as intellectual growth or social enhancement. It is balanced, too, within a single developmental area. For example, in facilitating physical development, activities should be employed to foster the use of both small and large muscles. In language arts, both speaking and listening skills merit attention. A well-balanced program permits both internal structuring of concepts (best epitomized by child-directed activities) and external structuring of concepts (as in teacher-directed activities). And finally, a good program balances individual liberty and social responsibility.

Not always, of course, will the balance be perfect. Teachers have different philosophies and different ideas of what is important. Children have different needs. The "chemistry" of a class—the way it operates as a total group—is so variable that a balanced program for one group will not be balanced for another of the same age. It is important, however, that the program not have a continuing and a deliberate imbalance and that it not slight important areas.

Planning a balanced preschool program is no easy task. For this reason, the following guidelines are suggested as a reminder for you to use when planning a program. The guidelines are not all inclusive but rather representative of worthwhile experiences. Neither are they presented in a hierarchy of importance. Each of them is significant. A balanced preschool program should provide these opportunities for children:

1. To succeed and to feel worthy.
2. To share in making decisions and in accepting responsibilities.
3. To develop values and behaviors consistent with democratic living.
4. To develop problem-solving skills.
5. To explore the natural environment.
6. To develop routines and habits that facilitate positive social living and enhance personal well-being (for example, sharing ma-

terials, cleaning up materials after their use, and washing hands before eating).
7. To be active and to rest, to interact with others and to be alone.
8. To improve communications skills.
9. To expand expressive skills in art, music, movement, and dramatic play.
10. To develop comprehensive sensorimotor skills (for example, acquiring large and small motor skills).
11. To establish conceptual foundations in mathematics, science, and the social sciences.

In a balanced program, at least two of the "opportunities" must apply to parents. Parents should have opportunities (1) to become educated about their children's development and their own major role in aiding that development, and (2) to participate in the preschool program. Because of the importance of these opportunities for parents, a later chapter is devoted to methods of enhancing them.

As this list of opportunities for children implies, a good preschool curriculum also establishes a balance between its long-range and short-term objectives. Each opportunity will not be available every day. On some days, only a few may be stressed. But during the course of the school year, all of them should be presented. If these opportunities for growth are all presented, and if their presentation is not biased in favor of only one or just a few of them, to that extent the curriculum will be balanced.

PLANNING FOR SPECIAL OCCASIONS

Every day in school is important. And every day requires planning if it is to be successful. But some days in a preschool are more unusual than others and may demand different planning. Two such days—the first day of school and the field trip or visitation day—are considered below.

The First Day of School. No other day fills new teachers *or* preschool children with more trepidation than the first day of school. The occasion is new to both of them—a day filled with hopes and fears, anticipation and dread. Older grade-school children have some experience and security with which to approach the first day of the school year. They have been there before. Similarly, experienced teachers may be keyed up before the first day, yet they too have lived through a number of these landmarks and know what to expect.

But for many of you and for your students, this will be a *first*, first day. Some preparation can ease your fears. If possible, children should visit the classroom and meet you prior to the opening day. Many schools have orientation days that accomplish this purpose. Ideally, orientation periods should be staggered to enable teacher, parents, and children to become acquainted on an individual basis. While the child explores the classroom, you and his parents can work with him or chat informally together. Visiting your students' homes prior to the opening of school can also help to put children, parents, and teachers at ease with each other.

If preentrance activities are not possible, perhaps some provision can be made to stagger attendance at the beginning of the year, so that a small group of children rather than the entire class begins school together. Different subgroups might attend on alternate days or at alternate times during the day for the first week or two of school.

If neither orientation nor staggered entrances is feasible, although the first day of school will be difficult, it will not be impossible if you prepare yourself for it. This may be the first time the child has been in a large group, the first time he has been away from his parents for a sustained period, the first time he has been in this strange, new environment, and the first time he has ever seen *you*. He may welcome school because he has heard only good things about it or fear school because he has heard little that is good about it. At the same time, if you are a beginning teacher, although you have been trained to teach young children and you know how important your work is, you have never had your own class, you may never have worked with parents, you are unfamiliar with the politics of the school, you are insecure about your own abilities, and you don't know the children. Considering this situation, it is amazing that first days succeed at all. But they do. So, chin up. Both you and your children will survive it.

You should try to achieve two important objectives on that first day: (1) establish rapport with the children and their parents and (2) create an affective climate that communicates to the children and their parents that school is a happy, secure, and exciting place to be. Implement plans with these objectives in mind. You might use cheery name tags, for example, to enable you to learn names quickly and associate them with faces. Children also enjoy the feeling of importance, of worth, associated with wearing the tags. Parents should be welcomed to remain for at least a portion of the day, observing or participating with their children.

Avoid a common pitfall in planning for the first day—overplanning. Many well-intentioned new teachers falter because they treat Day 1 like any other day and plan regular activities. This day is simply like no other. Some general confusion should be expected and allowed for in your planning. Many children will immediately wish to explore the room, to try out new materials and equipment. Let them. Prepare for this behavior by setting out a minimum of equipment—enough to intrigue yet not over-stimulate the children. Other children may be more reticent about participating. They will want to watch activities silently or to linger with their parents. Let them. Again, anticipating such a reaction, you should suggest that parents stay until their children feel more at ease about school. Otherwise, you can plan sample preschool activities (for instance, a short group-time during which you might teach a song or tell a short story, a short free-play period, and other simple but representative experiences). The specific activities you plan for this first day are, however, less important than the sense of order, acceptance, and warmth you convey in your own behavior and by the climate you prepare.

Field Trips and Visitation Days. Field trips and visits from resource people require different planning strategies. Too often these activities are used as time-fillers rather than as the important learning experiences they can and should be. Trips and visitations should be used to introduce, clarify, or extend concepts in a concrete, and, if planned well, highly enjoyable way. Whether children are taken into the community or community resources are brought to the children at school, you should plan the experiences with specific objectives in mind. You should prepare the children and plan with them for the experience. During this preparation, you can stimulate interests, introduce basic preparatory concepts, and give the children a short preview of what may be expected from the experience. Such introductory activities will make that experience a more meaningful and enjoyable one for everyone.

It is essential also that you meet and plan with resource people whether the experience will be a field trip or a visitation. The "logistics" of the experience—how long it will take, when it will occur, where it will occur—should be discussed and established beforehand. Most important, you should inform resource personnel about the interests, needs, and maturity of your children to enable them to plan appropriate activities.

Administrative details should also be handled well in advance of the experience. If a field trip is projected, you must enlist adults to provide adequate supervision of children. You will need to make arrangements also for notifying parents, receiving permissions from parents and superiors, transporting children, and arranging for any children who may not participate in the trip.

When you prepare carefully for field trips and visitations, they are more likely to be valuable educational experiences. You can extend these experiences by implementing culmination activities, such as discussions or art projects, which not only consolidate learning but also may lay foundations for future learning.

Teaching in a preschool is demanding work. To ensure that your program is systematic and well balanced, to know that your "special days" are also well provided for, takes time, energy, and imagination. Your rewards lie in your students' increased learning and development. And that is what good teaching is all about.

FOR FURTHER READING

Anderson, Robert H., and Shane, Harold G., eds. *As the Twig Is Bent*. Boston: Houghton Mifflin, 1971.

Association for Supervision and Curriculum Development (Early Childhood Council). "Guidelines for the Analysis and Description of Early Childhood Education Programs." *Educational Leadership*, 1971, 28:812–820.

Auleta, Michael, ed. *Foundations of Early Childhood Education*. New York: Random House, 1969.

Bloom, Benjamin S.; Hastings, J. Thomas; and Madaus, George F. *Handbook on Formative and Summative Evaluation of Student Learning*. Ch. 14. New York: McGraw-Hill, 1971.

Carswell, Evelyn M., and Roubinek, Darrell L. *Open Sesame: A Primer in Open Education*. Pacific Palisades, Calif. Goodyear, 1974.

Child Welfare League of America. *Child Welfare League of America Standards for Day Care Services*. New York: CWLA, 1969.

Evans, E. Belle; Shub, Beth; and Weinstein, Marlene. *Day Care*. Boston: Beacon Press, 1971.

Frost, Joe L. "Analyzing Early Childhood Education Programs: The Nature of Educational Objectives." *Educational Leadership*, 1971, 28:796-801.

_____, ed. *Early Childhood Education Rediscovered*. New York: Holt, Rinehart and Winston, 1968.

Hymes, James L. *Teaching the Child under Six*. Columbus, Ohio: Charles E. Merrill, 1974.

Kaplan, Sandra Nina; Kaplan, Jo Ann Butom; Madsen, Sheila Kunishima, and Taylor, Bette K. *Change for Children*. Pacific Palisades, Calif.: Goodyear, 1973.

Klein, Jenny W. "Making or Breaking It: The Teacher's Role in Model (Curriculum) Implementation." *Young Children*, 1973, 28:359-365.

Lavatelli, Celia Stendler. *Piaget's Theory Applied to an Early Childhood Curriculum*. Boston: Center for Media Development, 1970.

Leeper, Sarah Hammond; Dales, Ruth J.; Skipper, Dora Sikes; and Witherspoon, Ralph L. *Good Schools for Young Children*. New York: Macmillan, 1974.

Mayer, Rochelle Selber. "A Comparative Analysis of Preschool Curriculum Models." In *As the Twig Is Bent*, edited by Robert H. Anderson and Harold G. Shane. Boston: Houghton Mifflin, 1971.

Mills, Belen Collantes, ed. *Understanding the Young Child and His Curriculum*. New York: Macmillan, 1972.

Patterson, June. "Analyzing Early Childhood Education Programs: Instructional Procedures." *Educational Leadership*, 1971, 28:802-805.

_____. "Analyzing Early Childhood Education Programs: Evaluation." *Educational Leadership*, 1971, 28:809-812.

Spodek, Bernard. *Teaching in the Early Years*. Englewood Cliffs, N.J.: Prentice-Hall, 1972.

three

Working with Facilities, Equipment, and Materials

CRISIS IN THE CLASSROOM

Children are running from all directions to get to school. You hear your kindergartners shouting with joy as they enter the classroom and you know why they are so keyed up. Today snow fell for the first time this winter, and they know that a snowman will be attempted before the school day ends. You, too, look forward to the activity with the same joy and anticipation. Watching the snow dance as it falls to the ground (where, you note with pleasure, it is not melting), you think it will be a delightful afternoon.

Children hurry into the room, sharing your excitement. Just as you turn to help a child with his coat, you hear a ghastly crash accompanied by a terrifying screech—then silence. George, eager to join the class, has slipped on melted snow at the doorway and flown across the room, bumping his head on a table as he fell. The thought that this scene would be funny were it not real flits through your brain. George lies stunned and frightened. The class is hushed, muted at the sight of his head, which is bleeding profusely. Other children run in, their shouts of joy stopped abruptly by the sight of their injured classmate.

You stand paralyzed. Priding yourself on being so safety minded, you've often bragged silently that you've never had a drop of blood shed in your classroom. Well, you've more than made up for it now. Images of concussions and fractures flash across your mind and the sight of blood activates your senses. Quick, quick you must do something.

YOUR REACTIONS TO THE ALTERNATE SOLUTIONS

ALTERNATE SOLUTIONS

1. Act quickly and decisively. Ask the children to watch George while you run to the principal or nurse for help.

2. Clean George's wound yourself. There is no need to get the administration and parents involved over a simple fall. If George behaves normally during the afternoon, consider him and yourself lucky. Then forget the incident.

3. Have George's wound tended to by a nurse, the principal, or do it yourself if necessary. Even if it appears to be only a bruise, notify the administration and George's parents about the accident immediately.

4. Remain calm. Send a child for the nurse or the principal. Try to staunch the flow of blood. Do not leave George alone for an instant. Await help and advice on the problem.

DEMOLITION DERBY

You have been working with fifteen children enrolled in Head Start for several months. In some ways, you note a lot of progress, but in one area— the treatment of materials and equipment—the children have scarcely improved. They are generally destructive—pulling wheels off trucks, throwing and kicking materials, and otherwise abusing equipment until much of it is either damaged or destroyed completely.

You excused the abusive behavior during the first weeks of school, recognizing that most of the children had come from poor homes and owned few toys. You suspected that some of the children had never learned to care for or respect property. Since school began, therefore, you have taught them how to take care of materials. A few children have responded well, but the majority seems to ignore your instruction. You've reasoned with offenders, explaining that if they damage equipment, they and their classmates will have less fun with it. Still, no impressive changes of behavior have emerged. Withholding toys or play privileges from offenders momentarily stops the abuse of equipment, but it soon recurs. Similarly, just when you think that praise for proper use of materials has begun to work, a new string of abuse begins. You theorize that it is almost as though the children enjoy destructive "play" more than the constructive activities they might otherwise engage in.

As you survey the puzzles with missing pieces, the toy trucks with missing tires, the paraplegic remains of once full-bodied dolls, the trikes with broken spokes and mangled wheels, the torn costumes no longer usable for dramatic play, the doors unhinged and broken off miniature stoves and refrigerators, you feel yourself sinking into a state of depression and despair.

You hesitate to compound the problem by buying and introducing new materials until the children can learn to use them properly. At your wits' end, you ask yourself, What more can I do?

YOUR SOLUTION

YOUR REACTIONS TO THE ALTERNATE SOLUTIONS

ALTERNATE SOLUTIONS

1. Put all but a very few materials away. Introduce each new piece of equipment carefully, explaining that if the material is abused, it will be removed from the room. Then follow through.

2. Your materials are probably poorly constructed if they fall apart so easily. Purchase better quality materials in the future. The quantity of materials obtained may suffer, but you and the children are better off with fewer pieces of more durable equipment.

3. Allow only the nondestructive children to use new materials. Hope that their privileges and treatment of materials will be an incentive for other children to follow.

4. Remove and repair broken materials immediately. Keep all of your equipment well organized and in good repair, setting an example for the children. Act promptly when materials are abused by removing them from the offender.

5. Don't worry. Materials are meant to be used, not worshipped. Equipment is replaceable. Children are not.

6. Call a meeting with parents to discuss the problem. Ask them to work with their children to develop habits of caring for property, which will transfer (you hope) to the school setting.

7. Use the situation as a learning experience for the children. When a child damages material that he can repair, help him to repair it. You might also set aside a day every so often on which the entire class repairs and maintains equipment.

BANG! BANG! BANG! OR, IS DIN A SIN?

You find yourself shushing your kindergartners constantly even though you are opposed to this frequent restriction. In fact, you feel as though you are working in a library at times rather than in a room full of exuberant children. Why? Because your classroom is located immediately adjacent to the principal's office in the modern new school.

You have long since stopped trying to understand what possessed the architect when he placed the room in this location. You know only that it is a permanent arrangement. But the tiny sinks, interior lavatories, low blackboards, oversized room, and attached play yard are ideal for kindergartners. A month after you took the job, however, subtle complaints drifted back to you from the principal and her office staff. Comments such as, "Whatever was that boy yelling about this morning?" issued by office personnel, conveyed more than idle curiosity.

You don't believe your classroom is lacking discipline or control. In fact, early childhood teacher education students from the local university have been referred to your class as a model (you assume) of a good preschool program. Parents are seemingly pleased when they visit. Were it not for the unfortunate physical placement of your room, you believe even your principal would be entirely happy.

Today, however, climaxed the frustration you have felt all year. Much to your embarrassment, the principal walked in and personally remonstrated your children about the need for less noise. She was kind but firm about it, giving you a wry smile as she departed. The school day is now over and you don't know whether to cry, kick a table, become the martial teacher you despise, or go have a martini. But you do know that you have to do something.

YOUR REACTIONS TO THE ALTERNATE SOLUTIONS

ALTERNATE SOLUTIONS

1. You may have less control than you think if the principal and other staff members are so disturbed. Put yourself in their shoes. It is difficult to work with a constant barrage of noise nearby. Apologize at the next opportunity. Then revise your behavior and your program to assure more tranquility. Instead of suffering, the program may, in fact, improve.

2. Ignore the complaints and continue to work as you have been working. You were hired to execute a good preschool learning program, and some noise is to be expected in the process. You cannot change your teaching, your beliefs, or natural child behaviors in an effort to satisfy unreasonable complaints.

3. Discuss the problem with your principal. She may need to be educated about your beliefs and objectives. If necessary, gather support from educational literature and from your colleagues to defend your program. Suggest that the office be moved or your classroom be insulated to improve the situation.

4. Both you and the office staff are uncomfortable with the present arrangement. Discuss the problem with them and offer to take another room. Even if the room is less desirable, you and the children will be better off without the constant pressure that now prevails.

5. Ignore the incident. The principal is clearly out of bounds in acting so unprofessionally. If her behavior continues, take the problem up with her superior, go to the grievance committee of your local teachers' association, or make some other move to defend yourself and the integrity of your program.

NOW YOU SEE ME, NOW YOU DON'T

You have ended another day in the nursery school, where you teach fifteen four-year-olds. You have that run-down feeling and you know it's not the result of a vitamin deficiency. You're tired and frazzled from trying to supervise children in a facility that not only discourages adequate supervision but, in fact, invites disaster.

The nursery school is located in a small rented house. Three downstairs rooms have been given over to the school, each of them housing the abundant equipment and activity necessary for the success of the program. The problem is that the only access and the only visibility from room to room is through the narrow doorways. Oh, how you wish you could see through the walls! Because you cannot, accidents and fights continually erupt in the unsupervised areas. You have an aide to help you with the class, but even so, it is impossible for either of you to be in more than one place at a time.

You've been disturbed by the situation for quite a while, but today you decided something had to be done immediately. Phyllis came screaming out of an unsupervised room with a large welt on her forehead, which was caused, you ascertain, by her falling over a carelessly overturned chair. As you tend to Phyllis, you seethe with rage and frustration, knowing that her accident and the many others that preceded it would probably not have happened were the school better designed for supervising young children. You think morbid thoughts about accidents that could happen in the future, and you shudder. Enough is enough. It is time to do something about the problem. But what?

YOUR SOLUTION

YOUR REACTIONS TO THE ALTERNATE SOLUTIONS

1. Close off any rooms that cannot be properly supervised. The children are better off crowded a bit than open to mishaps.

2. Revise your program so that all of the children will work in an area under an adult's supervision at all times. Either station yourself and your aide so that children can move freely between your areas of supervision or schedule children to move between supervised areas at specific times.

3. Modify the existing physical structure. You need the space and should not let a few walls keep you from using it. Remove, cut down, or otherwise modify the walls so that you can use the facility safely and effectively.

4. Don't overreact. After all, accidents can happen in your immediate presence as well as in your absence. Try to move yourself and your aide around enough to keep abreast of the situation. Otherwise, live with things as they are. You're lucky to have a facility at all.

5. Look for other facilities immediately. Seek a facility that has the space and design necessary to carry out an effective and safe program.

CAN YOU SUCCEED IN TEACHING
WITHOUT ANY TOOLS?

When you accepted the kindergarten teaching position, your principal assured you that you would have a great deal of freedom to develop a program reflecting your own teaching philosophy and style. What he failed to mention was that you wouldn't have any instructional resources to carry it out.

You were appalled when you first saw what was to be your classroom. It was tiny enough to pass for a revamped storeroom. Worse, there was a sparsity of equipment in the room, only a few tables and chairs. You assumed—wrongly, it turned out—that other materials were probably on order or in storage someplace. The outdoor play area consisted of a small fenced yard gutted with holes and covered with dirt. A rotting tire and a rusting jungle gym were the lonely inhabitants of the yard.

One other kindergarten teacher works in the building. When you talked with her about the lack of resources, she was not overly concerned. Now that you know her better, you understand why: She is seldom concerned about anything besides her paycheck!

You also talked with your principal. His response was one of indifference and wonder about your "fuss." After all, what kind of equipment did you need to run a kindergarten program? He implied that since children "mainly play" in kindergarten anyway, the limited resources were probably better used for other grade levels. When you tried to persuade him differently and told him that you needed play equipment, readiness materials, and even a piano perhaps, he smiled and said, "I'll see what I can do."

It is now January—four months later—and apparently he is still "seeing" but not "doing." You are not only frustrated by the situation but impoverished and fatigued by it as well. You spend almost every weekend scrounging, building, or painting materials for your program. What is more, you have invested a goodly portion of your modest salary in materials and equipment. Yet you've barely made a dent in supplying the minimal resources you feel are necessary. Nor are your ambitious endeavors endearing you to your less ambitious colleague.

After another unsuccessful session with your principal, in which he gushed with platitudes but offered no help, you decide you must do something else to get your program rolling.

YOUR SOLUTION

YOUR REACTIONS TO THE ALTERNATE SOLUTIONS

ALTERNATE SOLUTIONS

1. Solicit help from your PTA and any other likely civic-minded groups.

2. Call a meeting of the parents to discuss the problem and to effect solutions to it.

3. Go to the superintendent of your school district. Tell him of your desperate situation and of the way your principal has responded to it.

4. Quit at the earliest opportunity. You will probably get little support from your principal and, without it, your program cannot succeed.

5. Live with the situation. It is the human dimension—you, the teacher— not the inanimate materials that makes a difference in the lives of children.

6. Educate your principal about the purposes and values of early childhood education. It may take some time and effort, but it is necessary if your program is to succeed.

WORKING WITH FACILITIES,
EQUIPMENT, AND MATERIALS

Nothing can be more frustrating than lacking the space and tools you feel are necessary to carry out an effective preschool program. The physical environment *does* influence the program you implement and, for that reason, you need to prepare it in the best possible way. You can directly influence learning and development in children by obtaining adequate facilities and by carefully selecting, maintaining, and arranging the equipment and materials you will use in the program.

PREPARING THE ENVIRONMENT: FACILITIES

The type of facilities needed for a preschool will depend to some extent on the type of program offered. A child-care program involving planning and preparing meals, for example, may necessitate more extensive kitchen facilities than those needed for a partial-day program. Presented here are some important general considerations for planning and obtaining facilities.

The amount and arrangement of space are crucial factors in preschool planning. Unfortunately, regulations quantifying space have been far more specific than those qualifying it, even though the quality or arrangement of space may be the more important factor for achieving the program's goals. For example, a building may have adequate square-footage, but the space may be so chopped up that it precludes adequate supervision. Similarly, an outdoor area, though adequate in size, may be fully paved and therefore unsuitable for climbing, digging, and other activities that require a soft surface.

Although you will probably work in a structure that was designed by someone else, you may be in a position to modify the structure or to participate in planning a new facility. In either case, the following basic features would be included in the ideal preschool facility.

1. Adequate interior and exterior space. Minimum dimensions of approximately fifty square feet per child for the classroom and roughly two or three times that amount outside.
2. Interior design that permits flexible and supervisable use. Movable walls, single-level floors, free access between classrooms, play yards, and bathrooms, multisurfaced flooring (a fully carpeted classroom is impractical for many "messy" activities), adequate provisions for media use (for example, window darkeners, handy electrical outlets, and so on).
3. Adequate systems for heating, cooling, lighting, and muffling sound in the facility.
4. Colorful, unbroken wall surfaces for display, chalkboard, and other instructional purposes.
5. Interior storage areas for materials and equipment, accessible to the children. Bookcases, cubbies or lockers, cabinets, and the like should be child-sized and movable. Additional storage for materials not in use or for the teacher's belongings should also be included.
6. Child-sized plumbing in each classroom or adjacent to it.
7. Space for parent-teacher conferences, teacher planning, care for sick children, and so on apart from the classroom. A single room could suffice.
8. Exterior design that is flexible and safe. Paved surfaces for wheel toys and construction activities; unpaved areas for climbing, digging, and other activities requiring soft surfaces; both sunny and shady areas to permit comfort during play at all times of the day; a roofed area to provide shelter from the elements on rainy days and to store equipment not in use, if separate storage facilities are not included; accessibility from classrooms, toilets, and the street; external faucets for water play, gardening, and so on; a fenced and gated yard.
9. Additional space, conveniently placed, for any support personnel and services to be housed within the facility (for example, the kitchen and the nurse's office).

PREPARING THE ENVIRONMENT:
SELECTING, ARRANGING, AND MAINTAINING
EQUIPMENT AND MATERIALS

You are likely to be involved in selecting, arranging, and maintaining a variety of educational resources. Many teachers feel least secure in this area, yet the quality, variety, and arrangement of these tools can influence the success of your program. Nothing is more frustrating to the young child than to have equipment that is difficult to use because it is broken, poorly located, too advanced for him, or in other ways inappropriate.

The task of selecting materials should begin with a careful analysis of what you presently have, to avoid costly duplication and to ensure that your inventory is balanced. Whether you are selecting items to begin a program or to supplement the stock of an ongoing program, you will probably not have much money to work with. Your first goal is to try to obtain a variety of equipment without sacrificing its quality.

Once you have established what materials you need, you should make a list of your priorities. (School budgets being what they are, you will seldom get everything you want.) The list should contain not only consummable items, such as pencils, crayons, and paper, but also nonconsummable equipment, that is, items having a long-use life such as hollow wooden building blocks. The latter items, which are more expensive and permanent, require careful selection. If you consider some of the following attributes *before* you spend your money, you are far more likely to be satisfied with your purchases.

1. *Appropriateness.* Be discriminating when you select equipment and materials. Choose only those items that meet the developmental needs of the children and serve the purposes of your program. You might ask yourself the following questions: Are the items too advanced for the children? Are they too unsophisticated? Will they produce growth, stimulate creative thinking, and provide enjoyment? Will they help achieve worthwhile goals?

2. *Durability.* It often pays to wait a little longer to buy a more durable item than to see good money wasted and frustrations developed by acquiring equipment that does not withstand the heavy use to be expected from active youngsters. Equipment must often withstand not only heavy use but also the effects of weather or crowded and otherwise inadequate

storage. You should evaluate the appropriateness of the design, composition, and finish of each item before you invest in it.

3. *Cost.* Although high-quality materials and equipment are generally expensive, cost is sometimes increased by unnecessary frills or "extras" that add little to the value of the item. In general, if alternatives are available, the sturdier and simpler item may not only cost less but be a more valuable addition to your inventory. Considerations about use-rate also enter into considerations of cost: for example, you should determine which of several items similar in cost will be needed and used more often.

4. *Safety.* Even the most innocent-looking objects can inflict damage if they are used improperly. You should examine potential acquisitions to determine any inherent dangers. Consider questions such as the following: Are the edges of the item smooth and rounded? Are moving parts securely mounted? Are nontoxic finishes used?

5. *Flexibility.* Because children are highly creative in their play, you will want to acquire materials that will stimulate imagination as well as materials designed for specific uses. A talking, wetting, burping, eating doll can hamper a creative "mommy," for example, in contrast to a simple, unmechanized baby doll whose activities are determined by the young child's changing interests and imaginative powers. Similarly, it is wise to select equipment that serves dual instructional purposes. Multipurpose equipment not only saves money but also precious space. The easel used by children for painting could be used at another time to display a colorful poster.

Most preschool programs operate on limited budgets. For this reason, you will sometimes have to try to obtain equipment and materials from "unorthodox" sources. Many a preschool teacher has earned a reputation as the village scavenger because of his or her digging into piles of wood at lumberyards, visiting surplus warehouses, or cajoling local businessmen to contribute unsold odds and ends to the program. Parents and community organizations may often make or contribute materials if they are asked. Even if you can afford commercially made materials, you can still use your enterprise and imagination to equip your classroom with a fine collection of educationally stimulating equipment on a modest budget. Persuasion, the ability to collect, salvage, and construct materials can go a long way toward filling your room with exciting and inviting happenings.

But excellent educational resources will not produce the best possible experiences for young children unless they are arranged for optimal and effective use. The arrangement of equipment can determine whether children develop behaviors that are autonomous or dependent, cooperative or aggressive. Preschool instruction is often organized around interest centers, which are equipped to support the developmental needs and interests of the children. Indoor interest centers for housekeeping, other dramatic play, block construction, creative art and music experiences, looking at picture books, and sensorimotor manipulation are among those common in preschools. You and your students may wish to create other centers during the year—perhaps a class "store," for example. Outdoor centers for climbing, using wheel toys, water play, gardening, pet care, sand play, and games are also representative of those found in many programs.

Arranging interest centers is often a trial-and-error process. You will simply arrange and rearrange your centers and other resources until you find a scheme that works best for you. Considering questions such as those listed below may save you some work and frustration.

1. Which arrangement will produce the best traffic patterns? If children are continually running into each other or into equipment, frustration, aggression, and physical harm can result, none of which is conducive to their development or your sanity. Consider arrangements that will enable children to work uninterruptedly and to move from one area to another without disturbing others. Interest centers and other activities located on the perimeter of the classroom or play yard often work most effectively.

2. Which arrangement will ensure the children's safety? Because the young child is curious and often unaware of danger, it is most important that he be supervised at all times. You cannot tolerate an arrangement that prevents adequate supervision and safety—children must be seen and supervised at all times. A peripheral arrangement of equipment will enable you to view the children with minimal obstructions. Any visual obstructions that are taller than the children, such as large, movable bulletin boards, should be removed. The boundaries of interest centers should be low enough to see over without denying the children a feeling of privacy. Activities requiring the use of potentially dangerous equipment—for example, cooking or woodworking—should be pursued only when the children are constantly supervised.

3. Which arrangement will be most logical? Logic is subjective—in the minds of teacher and students. Generally, though, it is more logical to

separate quiet activities from noisy ones. A music center makes better sense placed next to a block construction area than next to the quiet library area. Housekeeping centers often provoke more imaginative play when placed near costume closets, and block play might be placed near the truck area to encourage creativity.

4. Which arrangement will assure the most flexible use? Most preschool equipment should be movable. (The jungle gym is one exception that generally requires permanent mountings.) Even storage areas can be fitted with coasters to permit rearrangement when necessary.

5. Which arrangement will foster autonomy and initiative? Preschoolers normally strive to achieve independent and initiating behaviors. As their teacher, you should actively promote the development of these healthy behaviors by arranging equipment and supplies so that your students can select, use, and store them with minimal guidance. The less you are needed to perform these tasks for children, the better your arrangement. Low storage areas and systematically arranged materials can encourage your students' independence.

However obtained and arranged, educational resources need maintenance, a task that you should share with your children. Children are inclined to give materials the respect they deserve. If materials are broken, they tend to be unused or abused. In addition, children imitate adults in their care of equipment. If you appear to care enough to keep equipment in good shape, it is more likely that your students will develop positive attitudes toward maintaining equipment. Equipment that cannot be repaired or maintained should be discarded immediately. When maintenance is necessary, you might organize class work crews to aid you. Not only will children enjoy helping but they will share the satisfaction and responsibility of keeping classroom materials properly cared for.

FOR FURTHER READING

Berson, Minnie P., and Chase, William W. "Planning Preschool Facilities." In *Early Childhood Education Rediscovered*, edited by Joe L. Frost. New York: Holt, Rinehart and Winston, 1968.

Child Welfare League of America. *Child Welfare League of America Standards for Day Care Services*. New York: CWLA, 1969.

Dettner, Richard. *Design for Play*. New York: Van Nostrand Reinhold, 1969.

Evans, Anne Marie. "How to Equip and Supply Your Prekindergarten Classrooms." In *Early Childhood Education Rediscovered*, edited by Joe L. Frost. New York: Holt, Rinehart and Winston, 1968.

Evans, E. Belle; Shub, Beth; and Weinstein, Marlene. *Day Care*. Boston: Beacon Press, 1971.

Kaplan, Sandra Nina; Kaplan, Jo Ann Butom; Madsen, Sheila Kunishima; and Gould, Bette Taylor. *A Young Child Experiences,* Pacific Palisades, Calif. Goodyear Publishing, 1975.

Leeper, Sarah Hammond; Dales, Ruth J.; Skipper, Dora Sikes; and Witherspoon, Ralph L. *Good Schools for Young Children*. Ch. 22. New York: Macmillan, 1974.

Matterson, E. M. *Play and Playthings for the Pre-school Child*. Baltimore, Md.: Penguin, 1967.

Miller, Peggy L. *Creative Outdoor Play Areas.* Englewood Cliffs, N.J.: Prentice-Hall, 1972.

Project Head Start. *Equipment and Supplies.* Washington, D.C.: Office of Economic Opportunity, n.d.

Stanton, Jessie, and Weisberg, Alma. "Play Equipment for the Nursery School." In *As the Twig Is Bent*, edited by Robert H. Anderson and Harold G. Shane. Boston: Houghton Mifflin, 1971.

four

Working with Parents

ANYONE FOR SEX?

You arrived home this afternoon to find a message that Paul Richards' father had called and wanted you to return his call immediately. Worrying that something has happened to Paul, a member of your kindergarten class, you quickly dial his number.

Mr. Richards answers and launches into the following tirade: "What in the hell is going on in your class? Lately Paul has been playing house with his little sister and *he's* doing all the housework—even changing the doll's diapers. When I tell him men don't do such things, he says you said they do. Today he came home and told me that he might be a nurse when he grows up. Can you imagine? A nurse! Now, listen here, I'm a good father and want to raise my son to be a man, not a sissy. What are you trying to do with him, anyway? I intend to see that people like you stop influencing our kids."

You listen in a state of shock. What, indeed, have you done? Believing in equal rights for both sexes and in liberal role definitions between the sexes, you've tried to eliminate sexism in your classroom by teaching about men and women in a changing world. You've openly discouraged sexist social interactions among the children in the class. When boys or girls have excluded one another from play activities solely on the basis of sex, you've intervened. Similarly, you've encouraged children to pursue activities on the basis of their interests rather than according to traditional sex-role definitions. Boys wanting to work in the housekeeping corner, girls wanting to play with trucks have done so freely in your classroom.

Until now, you have been pleased with your program. Boys and girls seem to value each other for their personalities and abilities rather than selecting friends simply on the basis of their sex. But Mr. Richards is not at all impressed. What can you do to defend your position, and, perhaps, your job?

YOUR SOLUTION

YOUR REACTIONS TO THE ALTERNATE SOLUTIONS

ALTERNATE SOLUTIONS

1. Fight fire with fire. You are the teacher, the professional. Tell Mr. Richards where you stand and why. Discuss your program with him and suggest that he remove Paul from your class if he disapproves.

2. Get to know Mr. Richards better. Have him come for a conference to encourage mutual understanding. Try to calm his concerns by informing him about your purposes and invite him to observe the program to learn more about it.

3. See your principal tomorrow. If you have not discussed your views with him previously, do so now. Describe the problem and obtain his insights and, if possible, his support.

4. Call a meeting of all the parents to discuss the school's role in liberalizing sexist attitudes and behaviors. Other parents may be equally concerned.

5. Drop your approach. After all, Mr. Richards has a point. The family should be responsible for developing social values. Children will acquire sexual attitudes from their homes and from other nonschool contexts. Retreat fast. You're clearly interfering where you shouldn't be.

STOOD UP ON YOUR FIRST BIG DATE

You are working in an inner-city public school. When you took the job, you were worried about handling the many problems you'd heard were characteristic of urban schools. Thus far, your worries have not materialized. Although many of your students are disadvantaged—both socially and educationally—you think they have accomplished much in the first few months of school. Assuredly, many of them have a long way to go, lacking sufficient verbal and other skills necessary to succeed in school. But your students are good natured, anxious to learn, and thoroughly fun to teach. Having these qualities in their favor, you think their educational problems can be overcome.

Now, after much planning, you are ready for your first day of parent conferences. You sent notes home to the parents of your kindergartners, inviting them to come to talk about their children and assigning them conference times for this purpose. If the assigned time was not convenient, you asked the parents to request alternate times. The only response you received was one request for a change of conference time, so you assumed you would have a busy day.

You had carefully gathered samples of each child's work into a colorful folder decorated by the child. You had written yourself notes about important items to be covered in the conference and were really looking forward to meeting your students' parents. It would be exciting, you thought, to meet the parents and to share insights about their children with them. You even bought a new outfit for the occasion!

Well, it is now four o'clock and you have had conferences with only *five* parents, all of whom have children with few problems. You are dismayed and frustrated at the lack of parental response. This is a problem you had not anticipated. What can you do about it?

YOUR REACTIONS TO THE ALTERNATE SOLUTIONS

ALTERNATE SOLUTIONS

1. Send notes home again for the next conference day, but this time insist that the children return the notes with some kind of parental response.

2. Forget it. If the parents don't care enough to respond, there is little you can do. Parents who are really interested in their children will take the time to come for conferences. Those who are not, will not.

3. Assess the situation and talk it over with your colleagues. It may be that parents care but cannot or will not come to school for daytime conferences. Try alternative methods of communicating with them. You might ask your principal for released time to visit homes or schedule evening conferences which may be more convenient for parents.

4. Do not attempt formal conferences initially. Try instead to get parents involved on an informal basis. You might request occasional help from parents for classroom projects, schedule back-to-school nights, make telephone contacts, and so forth.

5. Seek a parent who is willing to act as an intermediary or liaison person to overcome reticence and pave the way to better communication between home and school.

TO READ OR NOT TO READ

"Why isn't my child learning how to read? The Johnson boy is learning to read in his class. All this class does is play, it seems. When do the children learn how to read?" This anxious but forthright parent is echoing the sentiments of others who have asked you about formal reading instruction in your kindergarten program.

You know how complex the question of formal reading programs in kindergarten is—how, on the one hand, some experts argue that children should be taught to read as soon as they are ready, even if that is in kindergarten, whereas other professionals maintain that a formal reading program has no place in the kindergarten because other values and demands are more pressing. You hardly have a theoretical consensus to guide you.

Anyway, you believe you know the needs of the children in your class and, from your observations, few of them are ready for a formal reading program. Furthermore, with twenty-five youngsters in your class, it would be difficult to devote much time to those few children who might benefit from a formal reading program without foregoing other valuable activities. This is not to say that your children are not being challenged: You engage them in what you feel is an excellent reading readiness program. Opportunities for children to listen, to speak, to discriminate sounds and sights, and to otherwise prepare them to read are abundant.

You are not happy about the parental discontent nor about the issue that has caused it. How might you deal with the problem and ease parental concerns?

YOUR SOLUTION

YOUR REACTIONS TO THE ALTERNATE SOLUTIONS

ALTERNATE SOLUTIONS

1. Call for a parent meeting to discuss the curriculum. Prepare a good case for your program and expect your professional opinion to be accepted. If possible, have your principal and other experts available to convince parents of the correctness of your approach.

2. Discuss the problem with your principal. Listen to his advice and apply it if it sounds reasonable.

3. Involve parents in developing the curriculum. Invite their participation in the classroom to enable you to have a more effective program as well as to educate them about the program. Conduct meetings or conferences to open up communication about the program. Be willing to act on appropriate suggestions from parents.

4. Develop a formal reading program for the youngsters who appear ready for it and *make* time for the activity. After all, readers have rights too.

5. Discuss the problem with your principal. Analyze together alternative solutions to the problem. The staff might be involved in determining whether another instructional organization—an ungraded structure, for example—might not be more effective for individualizing instruction in the school. Or explore means for implementing a formal reading program within the existing graded structure. Paraprofessionals, older students, or parents might be employed to help you meet the needs of all your students.

6. Do nothing. After all, there will be plenty of time for children to learn how to read in a formal program when they enter the primary grades. Don't debase the kindergarten curriculum by making it a watered-down first-grade program.

PROMOTION COMMOTION

The end of the school year is approaching for you and your kindergartners. It has been a good year, all things considered, and you have learned much. You'll miss the children, but nonetheless you long for a summer rest.

Today is your final conference day for the year, and Patty's mother, Mrs. Jones, has just arrived. Patty is one of two children who are somewhat younger and certainly less mature than the other children in the class. She exhibits extremely immature social behavior. At play, if Patty cannot have her own way she cries and runs to you for help. She appears to be totally unconcerned with readiness activities, her attention and interest flagging shortly after an activity begins. Results from standardized tests have reaffirmed your year-long observations: Patty's measured intelligence was in the low-normal range, and her social maturity was measured as markedly below average. She also scored at the bottom of the class in the reading readiness test given a few weeks ago.

During the conference with her mother, you recommend that Patty be promoted into a transitional first-grade class the following fall. Since your school has such a class, you feel fortunate in being able to select this alternative to a rigorous first grade which, you feel, would offer Patty only limited opportunities for success. Mrs. Jones does not agree. You listen as she expounds on Patty's brilliance. Patty needs the challenge of competition to do her best, her mother maintains. Finally, Mrs. Jones hints that the kindergarten program has really been too easy for Patty and, despite being shown evidence to the contrary, she insists that her child be promoted to the regular first-grade program. What is your response?

YOUR SOLUTION

YOUR REACTIONS TO THE ALTERNATE SOLUTIONS

ALTERNATE SOLUTIONS

1. Don't argue with Mrs. Jones. Simply reaffirm your professional opinion and maintain that you will submit Patty's name for the transitional program. It is Patty's future you are primarily interested in, not her mother's pride.

2. You are in a vulnerable position to "go it alone" in such a conference. Schedule another meeting and this time bring all the help you can get: the principal, the teacher of the transitional first grade, the school psychologist, if one is available. Mrs. Jones may be won over by a team opinion.

3. Listen to Mrs. Jones's side, then accede, if necessary. It is possible that Mrs. Jones knows her daughter better than you do. Further, Patty may have a maturational spurt over the summer months that would enable her to work adequately in the regular first-grade program. Besides, if Patty has problems in first grade, that teacher can take appropriate action.

4. Try to arrive at a compromise with Patty's mother. Suggest that Patty be enrolled in the transitional first grade with the understanding that she be moved into the regular first grade as soon as she appears to be ready for it.

The major social institutions charged by law and custom with the care and education of young children are the school and the family. To the extent that these two entities can form an effective partnership born of mutual concern for the child's welfare and nurtured by cooperative participation in his development, to that extent can the child's environment be richer than that created by either agency acting alone. Too often schools seem to view themselves as substitutes for the family, not supplements to it. At the other extreme are parents who either fear the school or are jealous of its influence. When both groups can work in concert, the child is the happy recipient of their cooperation.

Partnerships do not just happen; someone has to make the first move. For a variety of reasons, that person will probably be you, the preschool teacher. One goal you will want to strive for is parental involvement in planning, implementing, and evaluating the preschool program. A second, and equally important, goal is your involvement in guiding and supporting constructive child development practices in the home. Each of these goals deserves your best efforts.

Traditionally, parental involvement in American education has occurred in peripheral, mainly incidental, ways. Parents elect or serve on school boards, act as room mothers and fathers, attend PTA meetings. Greater parental involvement has been, perhaps, more common in preschool education for several reasons. Some programs, such as cooperative nursery schools, have traditionally valued and implemented parental involvement activities—parents working as policy makers, as teachers' assistants, as Saturday morning carpenters and painters. Such federally funded preschool programs as Head Start have also mandated and effected parental involvement. Today, these successful home-school partnerships are not only expanding upward to embrace the higher grades, they are also broadening to include preschools that are neither cooperative nursery schools nor

Head Start centers. The debate about parental involvement has now been replaced by questions about the extent of involvement and its implementation.

Similarly, the teacher's role in educating and informing parents has changed both in kind and in degree. Parents have always learned from the schools to some extent. They heard things about school from their children. They received progress reports. They attended conferences at school. A broader view of parent education has emerged, however. It involves the notion of regular and systematic efforts to educate families about child development and to initiate and encourage family behaviors that will enrich the environment in which the child develops.

These trends are welcome and, in large measure, inseparable. For example, when a parent serves on a planning committee or assists in maintaining school equipment, he or she learns about the school, its purposes, its constraints, its needs. When you as teacher visit with Johnny's parents to tell them about his progress, your mention that he is improving in his ability to share equipment both informs (educates) them and involves them in his development.

Moreover, the resultant partnership between you and the parents of your students can have benefits for you, for them, and for their child. They know things about their child that only parents can know. And you can gain much from their insights. Conversely, your broader knowledge of child development can provide the child's parents with general information that could be useful to them.

ESTABLISHING THE PARENT-TEACHER RELATIONSHIP

Various practices can help bring about the active and complementary parent-teacher relationships described above. The following suggestions provide a starting point but by no means exhaust the possibilities for establishing such relationships.

School Conferences. These may occur informally or be planned in advance and have specific objectives. Sometimes a few words exchanged between you and the parent in a brief encounter are adequate to keep both partners up to date and informed. Other times, regularly planned conferences may be necessary to discuss in detail various educational matters pertaining to the child, the home, and the school.

Home Visitations. To get a clearer understanding of the child, it is important for you to become familiar with the home environment and, if possible, see the child interacting within it. Home visitations are extremely helpful to some parents who might feel threatened by the more formal environment of the school. However, some parents are uncomfortable about home visitations. They may be poor and embarrassed by the physical environment in which they live, or they may be undergoing problems that they feel are too personal to share with you. Under no circumstances, then, should you ever make a home visitation without consulting with the parents in advance. If they appear reluctant or ill-at-ease about the visit, find an alternative idea.

Parent-Teacher Meetings. Parent-teacher meetings generally are planned by teachers and parents to achieve specific purposes. They can be used to discuss problems or aspects of the program, to develop materials, or to enable parents to get acquainted not only with you but also with each other. The meetings might often serve as useful forums in which you can provide suggestions for creating optimal home environments for their children.

Observations. Observing their child in the school setting can be very educational for parents. It enables them to see how the child relates to other students, to adults, and to tasks in a group situation. Parents can learn much from observing how you work with their child. You might suggest various things to watch for or, if appropriate, furnish a simple observation guide for their use. Often, discussing the observation afterward is helpful for clarifying questions the parents may have. In any case, parents should be urged to observe the program.

Direct Participation. If possible, parents should be encouraged to participate directly in the instructional program. The benefits of such participation accrue to all involved—to you, to the parents, and to the children. You and the parents become better acquainted with each other and can learn much from viewing how each relates to the child. When parents are able to work with their child and others in a teaching situation, they can gain insights into the goals of the program and the development of young children. You can be helped greatly by an additional adult aide, while at the same time learning from observing and working with the participating parents. And the children get increased attention from the additional adult help.

You may be fearful about possible confusion and complications resulting from parents' working in the program. With only rare exceptions, these concerns are unnecessary, as long as parents are informed about what to expect and what to do in the program. Prior to their participation, they should be instructed about the daily schedule and their precise functions. Generally, parents work as assistant teachers, carrying out activities under your supervision (for example, reading stories, supervising play). You might want to have orientation sessions during the year to explain the facets of participation. Otherwise, you must plan prior to and during the school day. This latter means is satisfactory provided that you do plan, and that parents know exactly what to do. Remember, you are trained as a preschool teacher. They are not.

Policy-Making Boards. Some preschools have policy-making boards on which parents and other lay persons serve. Your function on these boards is not unimportant, because your responsibility is to inform and advise even as theirs is to decide. These boards provide good opportunities for you and the parents of your students to become acquainted. You will also be afforded the chance to interpret your program, thus helping to educate the parents on the board. And certainly, their service on it is one of the more tangible forms of parental involvement in education.

Sometimes it may be difficult to make face-to-face contact with parents. Many of them may have occupational or personal responsibilities that prevent them from taking an active role in preschool affairs. Some parents may fail to appreciate the importance of such involvement. Sometimes parents feel threatened by schools and teachers as a result of ignorance, poverty, and prior negative experiences with these institutions. Because direct contact is important, you should make an effort to involve all parents. Meetings scheduled at the parents' convenience could increase parent participation in school activities and hence, parent education. Room mothers, parent aides, or other adults familiar with the community could serve as liaisons to involve parents. Reluctant parents may be introduced to the program in small but significant ways. For example, you might send a note home with a child suggesting that the parent contribute some inexpensive materials to the school. Other parents might be asked to accompany children on a field trip or to share a special skill or interest with the children.

There are other methods of keeping parent-teacher communications open. Occasional notes or regular newsletters can convey important and ongoing aspects of the program. Short telephone conversations can also advance the educational partnership. They permit you to casually share with the parent a special occasion at school: "Mrs. Jones, Jane printed her name for the first time today. She was so delighted."

The following guidelines can enhance the parent-teacher partnership, making it satisfying and educational for both participants.

1. Learn as much from parents as you hope they learn from you during parent-teacher contacts. Be prepared to listen as well as to speak.
2. Assume that a joint interest and effort exists in planning for the child. Think in terms of how "we"—you and the parents—can work together.
3. Take a positive approach. Be honest but encouraging in your reports to parents. Discuss not only the child's weaknesses but also his or her strengths.
4. Be professional without being preachy. Talk *with*, not at, parents.
5. Avoid discussing problems with parents in the child's presence.
6. Do not compare the child with other children.
7. Do not share personal information about a parent or a child with others unless it is within a professional framework (for example, for referral to another professional).
8. Avoid criticizing or otherwise placing parents on the defensive. Treat problem solving as an objective, joint effort.
9. Communicate regularly with parents. Don't save conferences for problems, thus reinforcing any negative feelings parents may have about schools. Parents need to know when things are going well in addition to knowing when problems arise. In fact, ongoing communication can keep many problems from developing.
10. Relax and enjoy the opportunity to work with parents. Realize that they may be as fearful and nervous about these encounters as you are. An open, sincere attitude can go far to dispel these initial fears.

When parent-teacher relations are established and carried forth with mutual respect, they can be among the more satisfying encounters in your professional life, and perhaps in the lives of the parents as well.

FOR FURTHER READING

Conant, Margaret M. "Teachers and Parents: Changing Roles and Goals." *Childhood Education*, 1971, 48:114-118.

Gordon, Ira J. "Parent Involvement in Early Childhood Education." *National Elementary Principal*, 1971, 51:26-30.

_____. "What Do We Know about Parents As Teachers?" *Theory into Practice*, 1972, 11:146-150.

Hess, Robert D., and Croft, Doreen J. *Teachers of Young Children*. Ch. 3. Boston: Houghton Mifflin, 1972.

Project Head Start. *Parent Involvement*. Washington, D.C.: Office of Economic Opportunity, n.d.

_____. *Points for Parents*. Washington, D.C.: Office of Economic Opportunity, n.d.

Saylor, Mary Lou. *Parents: Active Partners in Education*. Washington, D.C.: American Association of Elementary-Kindergarten-Nursery Educators, 1971.

Spodek, Bernard. *Teaching in the Early Years*. Ch. 13. Englewood Cliffs, N.J.: Prentice-Hall, 1972.

Thurlow, Angela P. "Parent-Teacher Communication." *Young Children*, 1972, 38:81-83.

Wilcox, Preston. "Parental Decision-Making: An Educational Necessity." *Theory into Practice*, 1972, 11:178-183.

five

Working with Staff and Administration

VOLUNTEER HELP? HELP!

As a busy Head Start teacher one summer, you were grateful to learn that two volunteers would be joining the program to help out. Little did you know! The volunteers were two irresponsible teen-aged sisters, Joan and Jean, who, it turns out, act more like the preschoolers with whom they work than like the adolescents they are. In fact, they sometimes appear less mature than the four-year-olds. But, you're in a bind. Their mother, who, you suspect, may be very happy to have her girls occupied during the summer days, is probably the program's strongest supporter. Having worked to get the program funded in the first place, she now drives for field trips and solicits materials and equipment.

During the last two weeks, you have tried to teach the girls exactly what they are to do in the program, but to no avail. They nod, giggle, and promptly ignore everything you've told them. Today you tried again to make good use of their presence by assigning each of them to supervise a group of children in an activity. Joan was to watch children walk across a balance beam, showing them specific techniques and standing by to prevent accidents. Jean was to supervise a workbench at which four children were busily embarked on creating cars, ships, and whatever else they desired from wood, nails, and other building materials. You had specifically instructed Jean to control the situation carefully lest accidents occur with the dangerous tools.

Moments later you see Joan trying to walk the balance beam forward, sideways, and, when she can manage it, backward. She is thoroughly enjoying playing on the beam while her charges drift off to more interesting and sometimes mischievous entertainments. Meanwhile, Jean has begun to build a ship herself, and a few children have stopped working to watch her. Behind her back you spot one child fighting with another over a saw, while a third child throws his project down in disgust because he cannot find the proper nails to complete it. Immersed in their own gratifications and games, neither girl appears to be conscious of what is happening around her.

You're furious and frustrated because you have two teenagers to care for in addition to the preschoolers. As you retrieve the saw, nails, and the wayward youngsters, you decide that you have had it. If this is volunteer help, you don't want any! What can you do?

YOUR REACTIONS TO THE ALTERNATE SOLUTIONS

ALTERNATE SOLUTIONS

1. Take the wandering youngsters back to each activity and have them begin it anew under your guidance. Teach the girls how to teach. Run through the activity; then have each girl try it alone until she achieves competence.

2. Bawl the girls out. Tell them to either shape up or ship out. You have enough to do to plan for fifteen four-year-olds without also having to plan for two immature adolescents.

3. Ask the girls to wait for another summer to volunteer their help. Tell them you appreciate their efforts but do not need their help at this time. Worry about what their mother says if and when she says something.

4. Ignore the problem. The girls will probably catch on to their roles from watching you in action.

5. The girls are obviously overly dependent on each other. Make up a reason to separate them. You might, for example, have them come to help on alternate days.

6. Begin an in-service training program immediately. How can the girls learn what is expected of them if you do not teach them?

GOOD MORNING, MISS ABERNATHY

Miss Abernathy is wonderful, an absolutely marvelous kindergarten teacher. Just ask anyone in the community—most of whom had Miss Abernathy as a teacher when they were in kindergarten—and they'll tell you how great she is. A teacher at your school for almost forty years, she is now teaching the grandchildren of her former students. And no one knows better how good she is than Miss Abernathy herself. The trouble is that you—and seemingly, you alone—don't believe it.

When you accepted this job (your first), you were told by the principal that you would be fortunate indeed to work with "Miss A.," as everyone calls her. "She's the other kindergarten teacher," he told you, "and has been here for years. She's really superb and I've asked her to work with you during your breaking-in period."

Apparently your "breaking-in period" is to take all year—or worse, to last until Miss A. retires—that is, if you last that long. Even though you're in separate classrooms, she knows about your every move. She insists that you approximate the schedule she follows, read the stories she reads, use the units she uses. Somehow—perhaps from some parents who are a bit disgruntled that their children are in your class and not in Miss A.'s—she learns of any deviations you make, any changes that might reflect your own teaching style and philosophy.

The problem is becoming unbearable. You're beginning to feel like a youthful carbon copy of Miss A. You feel thwarted, unable to decide anything on your own or to do anything spontaneously. What's making matters worse is that Miss A. just isn't all that good. She very obviously favors docile, well-dressed little boys and girls. And she's a rigid authoritarian under her facade of openness. Some of her methods are questionable. She regularly fills her "creative" art periods with coloring book activities, tracing, and the like. She moves her students little beyond rote mouthing of numbers and letters of the alphabet. And she is quick and vocal in her abuse of wrongdoers, shaming them loudly before their peers and assigning them to what she calls her "naughty nook."

But what can you do? Miss A. is direct in her insistence that you follow her lead. Discussing the problem with the principal won't help, since he thinks Miss A. is the greatest teacher since Socrates. She was, after all, his kindergarten teacher. You've considered quitting in midyear. Yet you do like your children and believe that if you were on your own, you could teach them very effectively.

YOUR SOLUTION

YOUR REACTIONS TO THE ALTERNATE SOLUTIONS

ALTERNATE SOLUTIONS

1. Be tolerant and tactful. Comply with whatever is expected of you until Miss A. leaves. Remember, you too may be a Miss A. someday.

2. Do your own thing. Stand up for your own beliefs and methods. You are not Miss A. If your principal and the parents cannot accept two kindergarten teaching personalities, that is their problem, not yours.

3. You should gladly imitate Miss A. You could do worse. She must be an exceptional person to garner the support she has.

4. Start looking for new employment. Your situation is too hot to handle and too difficult to change.

5. Confront your principal and Miss A. with your feelings. They may honestly believe they're helping you as you begin your teaching career. If they understood your feelings, they might respect you and behave differently.

YOURS, MINE, AND OURS

One of the things you looked forward to as you began your first job as a kindergarten teacher was the challenge of arranging materials and equipment in the best possible way. You had learned the importance of preparing an environment conducive to learning and safety. But you had never reckoned with the reality of sharing a room with another teacher, and especially one whose philosophy of education might differ so markedly from your own. You met your colleague during the preplanning session a week before school began and, after tactfully sharing pros and cons about how various pieces of equipment and activity centers should be arranged, you struck a compromise.

It is now November and you feel stymied. The sharing arrangement has been less than satisfactory for you. Your counterpart has steadily rearranged, deleted, and added materials and equipment to please herself. You have tried to be flexible, meeting the changes as a challenge. But the children are not nearly so indifferent. You spend much of your time digging out materials that are highly valued and used often in your class though not popular with your colleague, who continually stores them away again. You feel that the changes she is making in the environment are having a subtle and negative effect on your program, although you cannot pin the effect down to anything precise.

Last week, however, the change was no longer subtle. You came to school to find that the "circle area," an area of vacant floor next to the piano, which you found indispensable for story time, music, games, and large motor activities, had disappeared. In its stead were several rows of tables. These were in addition to those already present in adequate numbers, you felt, throughout the room.

You cannot tolerate the effect this new alteration would have on your program. Where will the children sit during story time? At the tables at rigid attention? Where will the children skip, dance, play games, and perform the many musical or movement activities you consider imperative for their development? Clearly, they will have to dance on the table tops unless you take some action. At this point, you are totally frustrated with the restrictions imposed on your program by the "sharing" arrangement, and you realize that your counterpart probably feels the same way. Since other facilities are not available, you must continue to share a room. Yet you know that something must be done if you and she are to survive the year together.

YOUR REACTIONS TO THE ALTERNATE SOLUTIONS

ALTERNATE SOLUTIONS

1. Meet with the other teacher and your supervisor to determine whether a larger room is available in your building. If so, suggest that a trade be made that would enable both of you to spread out a bit. In a larger room, you would at least have space for equipment for both of your programs.

2. Meet with your colleague and discuss the problem honestly. Try once again to reach a compromise that each of you could accept. If a compromise seems impossible, call in a third party to mediate.

3. Have the tables removed. Your colleague never asked your advice or permission before acquiring them. Why then should you consult with her before removing them? Act on your own in other matters also, just as she has. If you continue to submit meekly to her will, you will be hopelessly frustrated by June.

4. Meet with your colleague immediately and reiterate the original compromise. Explain your need for the open area and insist that either she remove the tables or that you will do so.

5. Don't make a mountain of a mole hill. Ignore or at least live with her changes. Room arrangements and equipment do not make or break a program. You, the teacher, do.

6. Plan to rearrange the environment on a daily basis to suit your own objectives. Inform your colleague of your plans and invite her to do likewise. It will mean more work for each of you, but the efforts will be well worth it if they improve your instruction and your temperaments.

7. Live with the situation as it is for the rest of the year. Work as well as possible around the obstacles but next year refuse to share a room with someone whose beliefs are in conflict with yours.

AN AIDE IN NEED OF AID

Gloria is a sincere, well-meaning classroom aide recently hired to assist you in teaching three-year-olds. And Gloria is helpful in many ways: she cuddles crying children, dries runny noses, supervises play, and generally appears to be a warm and competent person.

One day, however, you overheard her scolding a little boy in the bathroom: "Tommy, don't you go to the toilet when little girls are in there. It's naughty. Only dirty boys do nasty things like that. Shame on you. I'll spank you hard if I catch you again." Yet, sharing the bathroom is an acceptable practice in your class. Not only is it an innocent activity, you feel, but also an educational one for preschoolers, since casually observing each other satisfies their normal curiosities.

You are shocked by Gloria's outburst but decide to overlook it as a momentary and regrettable exception. On subsequent occasions, however, you hear her reproach other youngsters in a similarly abusive manner for behaviors that are not in any way abnormal or harmful. The more you observe Gloria and analyze the situation, the more you suspect that your middle-class value system and her lower-class values may be in sharp conflict. Further, Gloria's methods of dealing with child behavior are not always compatible with what you believe are sound educational practices. She is quick to damn and slow to praise. You hear too many "shames" and "naughties" and too few "good-for-you's" from Gloria. You wonder what the effects will be of such conflicting values and practices on the children in your class, who come from various socioeconomic backgrounds themselves.

You like Gloria and the children appear to love her, yet you wish to reduce conflicts of values in your classroom, which could be harmful to the children. How, you ponder, should you do this?

YOUR SOLUTION

YOUR REACTIONS TO THE ALTERNATE SOLUTIONS

ALTERNATE SOLUTIONS

1. Intervene immediately in the next confrontation of this kind. Handle the situation the way you feel it should be handled and hope that you become a model for Gloria. Continue in this manner and assess Gloria's behavior frequently to determine whether your modeling has been effective.

2. Ignore the behavior. Gloria's values cannot be changed at this point. She is entitled to them. Furthermore, many of the children who share her cultural background are used to her values and will not be harmed by her responses.

3. Talk with your board or director about removing Gloria from her position. She won't change and her behavior is damaging many of the goals of your program.

4. Plan and implement an intensive in-service educational program for Gloria. Give her opportunities to learn about young children and to develop behaviors that will promote healthy child development.

5. Tell Gloria that you want her to change her attitude immediately. Let her know that you disapprove of her behavior and expect a change for the better, or else!

NO MORE MS. NICE GAL

Betty teaches in the room next to yours and your kindergarten classes occasionally gather for movies and other activities. On a personal level, you find Betty a charming and likeable person, but on a professional level, you have begun to question her integrity. What started as a spontaneous request for a favor has blossomed into a continual infringement on your time and worse, become a difficult teaching situation.

One day, Betty knocked at the connecting door between your rooms and quickly asked if you would keep the door ajar and watch her class while she made an urgent telephone call. You graciously consented. You continued to consent during the following weeks while Betty left to carry out important missions which you suspect involved rest, food, and tobacco most of the time. Because your rooms are isolated at the end of a wing and a long way from the principal's office, you are seldom supervised and Betty's ventures appear to have gone unnoticed.

Finally, you told Betty you would not be able to help her out in the future because you could not supervise *two* classrooms of active five-year-olds. In so doing, you found your friendship considerably weakened. You were willing to suffer the loss in the hopes that Betty would reform. Now, although you are no longer asked to watch her class, Betty continues to leave it unattended at various times. You sometimes hear ominous noises next door and dread the possibility of an accident during her absence. What can you do?

YOUR REACTIONS TO THE ALTERNATE SOLUTIONS

ALTERNATE SOLUTIONS

1. Confront Betty with your concerns. Issue an ultimatum: Either she stays with her children at all times or you file a report on her truancy. You don't need friends like Betty.

2. Close your ears and eyes and mind your own business. You have your own class to attend to. Should a catastrophe result, at least attention will finally be drawn to Betty's negligence and appropriate action can be taken. Anyway, what goes on in Betty's classroom is the administration's problem.

3. Don't get involved in a confrontation with Betty. Go to the administration with the problem. Ask for their discretion in handling it so that Betty will not hold you responsible. After all, you may have to work with her after she is chastised.

4. Back down on your ultimatum. Offer to watch Betty's class again in the interests of her children's safety. It's better that *you* rather than the children be abused.

WANT TO EAT? BE SWEET

It is lunch time in the day-care center where you teach. As you pass a fellow teacher's room, you see her students happily eating one of their favorite meals: chicken and rice. A single child sits with only his milk before him. You know immediately what has happened. The child has misbehaved in some way and is being punished for it by missing his lunch.

The practice of withholding meals as a form of punishment is not uncommon at your school. If children do not behave, they often do not eat. You despise the practice and have never used it yourself. Until last week, you naively assumed that your director was unaware of it. Otherwise, would she not have stopped it? After all, most of your students are disadvantaged children who need all the nutrition they can get.

Because you are a newcomer hired only a few months ago, you have been reluctant to "rat" on your colleagues. But after some hesitation, last week you decided to speak to the director about the practice. Instead of being horrified by your news, she calmly replied, "It is up to teachers to use whatever discipline they find necessary. None of the children will starve. And they soon shape up when they know they will miss meals." Her response explains at least why the practice is so rampant.

You wonder whether parents know or even care about the situation. Of course, many of the children are too young to be very communicative about such things. Anyway, *you* know, and, although you need the job, you cannot continue to watch children being deprived of food they need. You consider your next move and realize that you have a problem: If you complain to the authorities or to the parents about the practice, your director and colleagues will no doubt deny that it exists. Then you will lose your job and the children will continue to go hungry. What, if anything, can you do under the circumstances?

YOUR REACTIONS TO THE ALTERNATE SOLUTIONS

1. Report the malpractice to your board of directors, the local board of health, or other appropriate agencies, even if it costs you your job. You don't want a job like this.

2. Do nothing for now. In a few months, make an anonymous telephone call to persons in authority—members of your board of directors or of appropriate local agencies. Describe the situation and identify the school, but do not identify yourself.

3. Live with the situation. The children will really not suffer as much as you think they will.

4. Continue to provide a model of good teaching and hope that your model is emulated. Otherwise, tactfully persuade your colleagues to try more effective and acceptable methods of guiding child behavior.

5. Discuss your feelings with the director. Forewarn her that unless the practice of withholding meals is stopped, you will take action to see that it *is* stopped. If she fires you or otherwise fails to stop the malpractice, follow through on your threat.

THERE WAS AN OLD TEACHER
WHO LIVED IN A SHOE

After a summer of rest, you looked forward to greeting your two kinder-garten groups this fall and beginning a new year of challenging experiences. It is now January and you feel less optimistic about the whole situation. Furthermore, you're worn out. Although the children are wonderful, there are simply too many of them. You talked with your principal about the problem early in the fall and he commiserated with you. According to him, the neighborhood had steadily been growing older, and everyone had assumed that the kindergarten enrollment would decrease again this year as it had for the last five years. In fact, a limit of twenty-five students per class had existed as a standard and was a reality until this year, when thirty-three children showed up for each of your two classes. He assured you that the increase was probably a fluke and that your enrollment would probably stabilize to achieve the normal load by January. If not, he would try to establish another class.

Instead of losing students, however, you have gained more until you now have thirty-six children in each of your classes. You feel that over-population in your classes is seriously affecting not only your health but the instructional program as well. You can easily see the effects of the overcrowding and they are entirely negative. Compared with other classes you have taught, the children fight more—defending their territorial and property rights—because the space and materials are not adequate for their numbers. Children bump into each other and battle over paints and blocks. You, too, are changed. Snack time makes you act like a harried waitress at a dime store lunch counter. You feel like a crowd-control man-ager or a drill sergeant rather than the facilitative teacher you want to be. You have to talk more loudly more often; some might even call it scream-ing. In total, you doubt that the children are learning much that is whole-some and you fear that you are about to lose not only your ideals but also your sanity unless something is done.

Today you speak with your principal again. He informs you of his awareness of the problem but states that there is neither space nor money for another class to be opened until the following fall. Then he solicits your suggestions for making the best of the situation.

How do you respond?

YOUR SOLUTION

YOUR REACTIONS TO THE ALTERNATE SOLUTIONS

ALTERNATE SOLUTIONS

1. Suggest that volunteers from the community be sought to help in the classroom, if money is not available to buy additional instructional aid. The volunteers might be parents of children enrolled in the program as well as other interested adults.

2. Suggest that children from the upper grades be released to work as classroom aides on a regular basis.

3. If money is available, suggest that paraprofessional aides be hired to improve the instructional program.

4. Suggest that attendance be staggered until the crisis is over. Half the class could attend on Mondays and Wednesdays, the remaining half could attend on Tuesdays and Thursdays, and all could attend on Fridays.

5. Suggest that three shorter sessions, each perhaps two hours long, be implemented for the remainder of the year. A third of the entire kindergarten group—twenty-four students—would attend each session.

6. Live with the situation as it is. It is too late to change much this year. The children, too, might react unfavorably to sudden changes at this point. Next year, suggest that the administration be more adequately prepared than it was this year.

WORKING WITH STAFF
AND ADMINISTRATION

To the uninformed lay person, teaching often appears to be a lonesome profession in which the teacher spends all of his or her time with children, in a world devoid of other adults. In the premise of an old story, the teacher even begins to think and talk like her youthful charges. The joke portrays a first-grade teacher of many years' experience (much of it using reading primers) who buys herself a new car. Shortly thereafter she finds that its fender has been crumpled by a hit-and-run-driver. "Oh, oh, oh," she exclaims, "look, look, look. Damn, damn, damn!"

In fact, you will discover early in the game that your work involves frequent contact with other adults—parents (discussed in Chapter Four), paraprofessionals and volunteers who assist you in your classroom, fellow teachers, school administrators, support workers, and community health and welfare personnel. Of course, the hat you wear most often is that of the teacher of young children, but you have other roles to perform as well. These other roles can affect your work as a teacher in significant ways.

WORKING WITH PARAPROFESSIONAL
AND VOLUNTEER STAFF

The children in a preschool program do not sit quietly in the orderly rows that their older brothers and sisters may occupy. They are very active. And they are young. Further, instruction for them is often highly individualized. Because of their activity and their youth, they need more adult help and supervision than older children require. Yet schools can seldom afford to employ only professionally trained and certified adults. Therefore, they often hire paraprofessionals—adults who have some training in education or are acquiring it as they work with you. Working under your leadership, paraprofessionals can become highly effective members of the teaching team. In well-functioning teams, it is often difficult to distinguish between the head teacher and paraprofessional staff members.

Not all teams function well, though. In some preschools, paraprofessionals do little more than check attendance and clean up after the morning juice break. Human potential is badly underused in such situations. Additionally, the children are short-changed by receiving less guidance and stimulation than they would get if the adults were more broadly employed.

It is part and parcel of your teaching role, then, to provide the leadership necessary to make wide and efficient use of any paraprofessional aid you are fortunate enough to have. If you believe that the paraprofessional is a valuable member of the team, that he or she can bring a special teaching style, a knowledge of the community, and an exciting personality to the team effort, you will work to achieve a cooperative rather than an authoritarian mode of leadership. The paraprofessional should be included in all the aspects of the program in which you think his or her talents will make a contribution.

The paraprofessional may have minimal training or none at all, and will be working with you as a method of acquiring increased competence. In these instances, your role becomes teacher trainer, in part. Much of this training will be informal, occurring indirectly during your daily work together. Sometimes it may be more structured, if you plan specific learning experiences for your aide. Letting the aide handle the story session after you have talked about it together is a way to test his or her competence in that activity and yours as a trainer of teachers. You should always be open, willing to answer questions about your teaching, about why you planned for a certain activity or handled a certain student in the way you did.

In addition to the paid paraprofessionals just described are the unpaid volunteers whose services you may employ. You may try to get volunteer help in areas in which neither you nor your regular staff feels particularly strong: music or art, perhaps. Older members of the community can provide the multi-age contacts that many of today's youth lack in their relatively homogeneous neighborhoods. Men as volunteers, especially, can help alter the traditionally female stereotype of the preschool teacher.

Whatever the nature of the paraprofessional or volunteer help you have, it is important that you (1) treat aides as co-workers, not as servants, (2) try to capitalize on their special skills and help them improve in areas in which they are weak, (3) remain open to their suggestions and responsive to their needs, and (4) all work together as a team. In these ways, the chances for the success of your total program will be substantially enhanced.

WORKING WITH FELLOW TEACHERS

Preschool teachers often work with other teachers. Sometimes teachers work together in a vertical arrangement: You will work with teachers from the upper grades to ensure that the total program for the school or even for the school district has continuity, coherence, and interrelatedness among the grade levels. More often, you will work with other early childhood educators. Together you may be charged with the responsibility of evaluating the present curriculum or perhaps revising it. Or you may simply meet periodically to share teaching techniques and problems and to discuss issues related to your teaching.

Team teaching is a particular type of cooperative relationship in which you and one or more other teachers work together on an assigned and regular basis. Typically, these other teachers will be fellow preschool teachers, although some schools have vertical teams of perhaps a kindergarten teacher, a first-grade teacher, and a second-grade teacher all working together with the same large group of students. Team teaching provides the opportunity for shared planning and problem solving. It increases the number of adults whom a child may think of as "teacher." It expands the opportunities for altering sizes of groups and for providing individual instruction. For example, one teacher in a team might spend most of a morning with one student while the other two teachers work with the rest of the group.

Yet team teaching can create problems. It demands joint planning, which is more time-consuming than independent planning. However, this planning is often better planning, since several teachers focus on the questions of objectives, activities, and evaluation. It also demands some compromise, some give-and-take, if the team is to work harmoniously together.

Many opportunities exist for dynamic professional growth when you and your colleagues are able to communicate and to work compatibly together. Although personal teaching styles and philosophies frequently differ, the team effort—defending ideas, compromising on issues, sharing techniques and materials—can help produce teachers who are individually more competent because they have been members of a cooperative relationship. In teaching as in other areas of human endeavor, two heads are better than one. When professionals respect each other, when they tolerate judgments that differ from their own, when they strive for consensus on important issues, when they cooperate to serve the interests of children, then mutual stimulation and creative responses to challenging problems can and will emerge.

WORKING WITH ADMINISTRATION

Unless you are teaching and directing a program yourself, you will probably work under the supervision of a principal or director. Your relationship with this person can be a determinant of your success as a teacher. His or her function is to stimulate and support you in your teaching efforts. Your director is the leader in school-wide program development. Additionally, the director controls budgetary and other resources, hires, promotes, and fires employees. It is this last duty—dismissing teachers when necessary—that often causes disharmony between teachers and administrators. If you see your supervisor as a threat to your job security, if he or she acts more as a critic of your work than a facilitator of it, then your working together may not produce happy or beneficial results for either of you.

It is in your best interests, therefore, to try to take a positive view of what you can gain from and offer to the relationship between you and your supervisor. Assume, and operate under the assumption, that he or she is there to help you. If you have ideas you would like to try, problems you wish to discuss, materials you need to obtain, go to the supervisor. This person can be an extremely valuable instructional resource. Similarly, if the director solicits your help or knowledge, offer it willingly and honestly. Your supervisor needs and wants your understanding and cooperation every bit as much as you need and want the understanding and cooperation of your supervisor.

WORKING WITH OTHER IN-SCHOOL PERSONNEL

A number of adults who work in schools do not teach or work directly with children. For some of these workers—secretaries, custodians, cooks— their lack of structured and assigned contact with children may make them feel less valuable. And worse, some teachers aggravate these feelings by acting as if they, too, believed that these workers were unimportant. In fact, they are very important to the total school environment. Schools in which the janitors, the office workers, and the kitchen staff are believed to be valuable members of a total team effort are likely to be better schools than those in which the noninstructional staff members are ignored or even abused.

You should make every effort to cooperate with these people, not patronizingly but sincerely. Whenever possible, you should consider their responsibilities when planning your program. For example, to ask the secretary one morning to call fifteen parents to secure permissions for a field trip—and to do so by noon—reveals not only your lack of advance preparation but also your lack of concern for the secretary's responsibilities. She does, after all, have her own regular duties to perform. It is especially important to thank these workers when they help out. The kitchen employees who spend extra time preparing cupcakes for your evening meeting with parents, the janitor who repairs the broken teeter-totter, these people deserve your appreciation. Cooperating with them will pay dividends.

WORKING WITH OTHER PROFESSIONALS

Personnel from health and welfare fields often work with preschool youth and their families to provide health care and social services. These workers may frequently join with the preschool teacher in a cooperative relationship. You may discover some of your relationships to be with nurses, social workers, psychologists, doctors, and other professional personnel. Sometimes you will make referrals to these people, perhaps informing them of health problems or family difficulties that may be impeding a child's progress in school. At other times, you may be the person whose professional judgment is solicited by a nurse or a social worker who may want information or advice from you about Janice or Johnny. You should try to foster the development of such cooperative relationships or, if the lines of communication are already established, try to ensure their continuance.

This chapter has discussed your working with other adults in cooperative ways. These are important aspects of your job as teacher, perhaps less visible than your actual teaching, perhaps less time-consuming, but important nonetheless. It is vital to the success of the entire program that you do your share to keep the cooperative venture of education functioning smoothly.

174

FOR FURTHER READING

Anderson, Robert H. "Schools for Young Children: Organizational and Administrative Considerations." *Phi Delta Kappan*, 1969, 50:381-385.

Combs, Arthur W. *The Professional Education of Teachers.* Boston: Allyn and Bacon, 1965.

Enzmann, Arthur M. "Developing New Teaching Teams." *Childhood Education*, 1970, 47:131-134.

Evans, E. Belle; Shub, Beth; and Weinstein, Marlene. *Day Care.* Chs. 7-9. Boston: Beacon Press, 1971.

Hodges, Walter L. "Analyzing Early Childhood Education Programs: Administrative Considerations." *Educational Leadership*, 1971, 28: 806-808.

Lally, J. Ronald; Honig, Alice S.; and Caldwell, Bettye M. "Training Paraprofessionals for Work with Infants and Toddlers." *Young Children*, 1973, 28:173-181.

Litman, Frances. "Supervision and the Involvement of Paraprofessionals in Early Childhood Education." In *As the Twig Is Bent*, edited by Robert H. Anderson and Harold G. Shane. Boston: Houghton Mifflin, 1971.

Project Head Start. *The Staff.* Washington, D.C.: Office of Economic Opportunity, n.d.

_____ . *Training Courses and Methods.* Washington, D.C.: U.S. Department of Health, Education, and Welfare, n.d.

_____ . *Volunteers.* Washington, D.C.: Office of Economic Opportunity, n.d.

Spodek, Bernard. "Staff Requirements in Early Childhood Education." *Early Childhood Education* (The Seventy-first Yearbook of the National Society for the Study of Education, Part II), edited by Ira J. Gordon. Chicago: NSSE, 1972.

te Due